T0193887

An EXPRESSION of LOVE
Told in Poems

DAVE ROUHIER, The Cowboy Poet

authorHOUSE

AuthorHouse™
1663 Liberty Drive
Bloomington, IN 47403
www.authorhouse.com
Phone: 1 (800) 839-8640

Published by AuthorHouse 10/08/2019

Scripture quotations marked NIV are taken from the Holy Bible, New International Version®. NIV®. Copyright © 1973, 1978, 1984 by International Bible Society. Used by permission of Zondervan. All rights reserved. [Biblica]

Scripture quotations marked KJV are from the Holy Bible, King James Version (Authorized Version). First published in 1611. Quoted from the KJV Classic Reference Bible, Copyright © 1983 by The Zondervan Corporation.

ISBN: 978-1-7283-3096-9 (sc)
ISBN: 978-1-7283-3094-5 (hc)
ISBN: 978-1-7283-3095-2 (e)

Library of Congress Control Number: 2019915926

Print information available on the last page.

This book of poems is dedicated to my two "Angels", Robin and "Happy". The love and inspiration they have given me has literally transformed my life. They allowed me to find myself and to determine why I was put on this earth. I will be eternally grateful.

> **You are the sum of your reactions to**
> **the things that you experience."**
> *– Dave Rouhier – 1985*

A very big thank you goes out to Margaret Clark-Mayfield, Diane West and Bucky Steffen for their part in doing the illustration work, the cover for this book, the web sites, as well as many other tasks I assigned them to do. The quality of this book would have been greatly compromised without their loving help.

Note: A number of these poems contain stories and parables spoken by Jesus and taken from various Bibles. In order to give the poems continuity, it was necessary to change some of the words. However, great care was taken to make sure the meaning of what was said survived intact. If you have any questions, consult your own Bible.

Preface

This is a book of love and life. What is love? I have explained it in these poems: love for your mate or sweetheart; love for your parents and siblings; love for humanity; love for nature; and most of all, love for God. Along with these are poems about life situations. They will open your mind and touch your heart. The topics include poems of honesty, kindness and peace of mind to name a few. Love, and peace of mind, come from the deep stillness within yourself. Love is a facet of your Being, inseparable from whom you are. Inside this stillness is The Christ within, and the truth that God is True Love.

True Love can be defined as the expression of the oneness of yourself with all of creation; the knowing that when you meet someone, or something, you are meeting yourself.This place within is where wisdom, knowing and truth are also found. There is a very deep abiding peace flowing from it. It has no shape, no form, but is who you are at your deepest level.This place contains infinite love because it is God within. It is eternal and never changes. It is consciousness itself.

Your greatest source of Love, Joy and Peace is always within yourself. Peace is not found by rearranging "things" in your life, but by discovering who you are at your deepest level. These poems are cause to invoke emotions. Let them take you to that place deep within yourself where True Love and Peace reside. My greatest wish for you is that you too will experience the Love, Joy and Peace that dwell within you, drawn out by these poems.

The story behind the poem: I had been writing a novel, inspired by "Happy," and had been up since 3:00 A.M. It was now about 10:00 A.M. and I needed a break. So, I went downtown for a cup of coffee. I was the only one in the place. As I sat there, I was thinking of the words I was using in the novel that I was writing. This poem just came to mind, and I wrote it on the back of a napkin.

Words

Words have power, persuasion, love in them
Words can heal, or even cause great pain
You can touch, or be touched, by a word
Even with God, first there was "The Word"

When you pray, you touch God with words
When you sing, you give voice to your heart
Your soul cries out because it can not speak
Thoughts and actions give voice to your soul

The story behind the poem: I have always felt blessed by this ability to write. I know where it came from, and I know why. Now I just write when I am inspired to do so.

The Spirit

Seems The Spirit moves me as I put down my thoughts
Puts the very words into my mind for that which I sought
It isn't very much work but loads of fun, don't you see
It's so wonderful to have the Holy Spirit looking out for me

Sometimes when I write the poems that I do I'm amazed
Where do the words come from, my mind was in a haze?
When it's all completely finished, and I read it all out loud
Must give credit to The Holy Spirit, no reason to be proud

This is all new to me within a few years, it seems
That God wants me to author poetry, as His heart deems
Wants me to touch others in a very kind and gentle way
And speak to them in rhymes about what He has to say

The rewards that I reap might be modest, or quite ample
By making a difference in peoples lives they can sample
Most of the poems have a lesson that you should learn
They might just help you decide which way your life to turn

The story behind the poem: When I was a youngster I went to St. Mary's Catholic school; eight years in grade school and another four years in high school. We were taught by sisters of The Holy Name. They had a lot to do with forming who I am today. I dedicate this poem to them and their good work.

What You Become

It's not so much what you get for that which you do
As it is for what you become, by seeing it through
A job filled with joy, compassion, caring and such
That helps other people with their lives is worth much

Feeling good about yourself and that which you do
Is part of the ticket that will get you to heaven too
Working all day helping those that are less gifted
Sends you home, warm inside, with your soul lifted

Now isn't that a better way to spend your life?
Instead of going through every day filled with strife?
Our days are numbered while we are on this earth
You should be working for eternity from your very birth

A hundred years of life divided by eternity is zero
Yet it will separate all the losers from the heros
So, if getting to heaven is on your priority list
Better not spend your time with your soul at risk

The story behind the poem: As I continued my search for the love of my life, I wondered how I was going to tell her who I was. At 3:00 A.M. I woke up with this poem going through my head. I had my answer.

Who am I?

I am your shadow on a bright sunlit day
And the breeze kissing your tears away
I am the bright cloud in the glorious sky
That makes you ponder and wonder why

I am the falling rain that cools you down
Puts a smile on your face, never a frown
I am the small lake in the mountains up high
Takes your breath away, makes you sigh

I am the rainbow seen at Mill Creek Falls
Cradling the thunder, your name it calls
I am the mighty Rogue rolling to the sea
Wishing two became one of you and me

I am a man wanting to experience it all
Find that perfect woman and really fall
I am a real cowboy with a heart so true
Looking for my soul mate, could it be you?

8

The story behind the poem: I was in the Nevada desert, car broken down, no money, no gas. My hip was out of place and I was in a lot of pain. Didn't have any idea how, or when, I would ever get back home. So, I just started walking. I walked headlong into an attitude adjustment. "Seek and ye shall find."

Rusty, Old Nails Three

I was walking down an old dirt road one summer's eve
Had a real bad day; my troubles didn't want to leave
Looked down and saw it there partially hidden in the sand
A rusty, old nail; square; kind used to impale His hand

Went a step or two farther and then found two more
Had a very eerie feeling that went right to the core
As I held them in my hand, heard a great cry of anguish
Realized Jesus paid the price; on the cross He languished

Lance pierced His heart; from rusty, old nails blood poured
He died with love in His eyes that my soul was restored
Troubles faded far away like they were never any bother
Just had to put my faith in Him, and also His Father

Now, whenever I have a problem, or way too much stress
Just reach inside my coat pocket and those nails caress
They remind me of Jesus, who cleansed my soul for free
Troubles bother me not; 'cuz of those rusty, old nails three

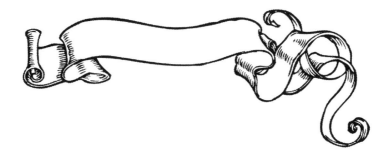

The story behind the poem: True love is all about surrendering yourself to someone. The more you surrender, the more love you are capable of giving and receiving.

Soul Mates

Soul mates we are, that's ever so plain to see
First time I saw You, You looked inside of me
I do not understand the power that You have
To heal all my wounds with Your magic salve

Heard You call to me; it was as clear as a bell
That You might save my soul from eternal hell
Your glory is astounding, there for all to see
But I see the love inside that's comforting to me

I love You as no other, no never, not ever before
I will just have to wait to see what's in store
I now see how this will all come to an end
And my soul to heaven You will most surely send

From dust You made me, to dust I shall return
But not before Your commandments I have learned
Total surrender: what You always expect of me
So that I may spend forever, with You, in eternity

The story behind the poem: A publisher told me I had to have a four-color book, and be sized 5"x7". I didn't want to use color because it would overwhelm the poems. I didn't want it 5"x7" because the print would be too small. Besides, this is a book about love and life, which is many shades of grey anyway, just like the book.

B.I.B.C.E.
(Basic Instructions Before Leaving Earth)

Bibles there are, mostly done in black and white
Tell of God's Word, about what's wrong and right
It is no secret why black and white was chosen
Words are cut into stone, as if for all time frozen

Color would distract from the message of the book
Your eye would see the color, your heart not to look
The message is very simple, the same as the cover
He teaches us to love, around Him we should hover

For my book I have chosen many shades of grey
Because the life we live can easily lead us astray
Tried to make it simple and right to the point of life
That you may learn from it, avoid some of the strife

It may not sell as well as the glitzy, colorful version
Those buying get the message without perversion
The meaning here is not to make money as an end
But to open your heart so to heaven He will send

The story behind the poem: Well, another song on the radio inspired this poem. I can't help it. I just see things differently than most, I guess.

I Love You This Much

"I love you this much." He was heard to say
As He hung on that cross most of the day
There are those of you who don't even care
And eternity in God's heaven you will not share

To love this much we must all be willing to do
With everyone you meet that loves you too
Even those that rebuke and slander your name
Worthy of your love, should be treated the same

Heard it said: "Do unto others as they do to you"
At times must just love, no matter what they do
True love is all consuming, doesn't ever go away
In your heart, mind and soul, will make your day

He was willing to die for all of us on that cross
Don't we owe it to Him to save our soul from loss?
The funny thing is, love given keeps returning
It will end up with Jesus, for it He is yearning

The story behind the poem: I have always called Robin and "Happy" my two "Angels." They are twins, and the youngest of seven daughters their parents had.

My Angel

An angel you surely are, I have no doubt
Sent by great Saint Jude to sort me out
I look into your eyes and see your soul
Filled with God, soft as a newborn foal

You have done miraculous things for me
Opened both my eyes so I may see
Now I know my calling at very long last
The reason I am here is not for my past

I am a guided spirit who's shown the way
And pray I am worthy of heaven someday
My heaven on earth revolves around you
How did I get so lucky? I don't have a clue

You have touched my life as never before
It makes me wonder what else is in store
The end the beginning, beginning the end
The ring of life allows your heart to mend

The story behind the poem: I was driving my cab one day, doing my job, when this came to me. I began to realize what my real job was, so I wrote this poem.

God's Special People

God's special people ride in this yellow cab of mine
I take them to and from most all of the time
Some are blind, but it is amazing what they see
Some have limbs torn and twisted like old oak trees

Then there are those whose minds are all but lost
They have hearts of pure gold, but at what cost?
They try to make friends the best way they can
When all they need is a caring and helping hand

A very few years ago, just before Christmas it was
Read of a five year old, a new tricycle he would love
The problem was a special tricycle he would need
Because he was crippled, his calling I would heed

Gave his mother $2,000 to fulfill his only dream
Santa would bring joy to both of us, it would seem
I never met the boy, I don't even know his name
Christmas morning tears of joy would fall like rain

The story behind the poem: I have a very keen insight into people. On rare occasions I can see their auras. Was in hope some might see mine as well.

Look Inside

The most beautiful view you should ever want to see
Is to stand outside yourself, and look in, if it could be
If you were to see clouds, angels, rainbows and such
Then you would know God your very soul has touched

When the beauty inside shines like the Northern star
It will outshine the beauty seen outside by so very far
Some people can't even begin to hold all that inside
Comes out as a rainbow colored aura they can't hide

Have known three woman that had an aura such as this
The minute you enter the room they're very hard to miss
Fell in love with one of them, was mesmerized by the glow
Want to spend the rest of my life encased by such a show

The blending of two bright auras, such an incredible sight
Like a Three D rainbow of color startling the still night
Would be match made in heaven if my aura she could see
Just take those sun glasses off, find a rainbow aura in me

The story behind the poem: I had been praying to Saint Jude a lot. He is the patron saint of impossible causes, and it was fitting for this situation. I decided to write my own prayer and make it a little more personal.

Prayer To Saint Jude

Oh dear Saint Jude, please hear my humble prayer
That she might learn to love me, our lives to share
I know that her love I don't even begin to deserve
But you are the worker of miracles, the one I serve

I have been praying to you for a very long time now
Miracles you have worked, but don't even know how
I have been on the receiving end of more than a few
I know that you work for Jesus, the one perfect Jew

Please, if you can but handle just this one more plea
You would make my day, indeed the rest of eternity
I have nothing I can offer her, only my humble self
She's my heaven on earth, all I'll ever need of wealth

I will pray your prayer nine times each and every day
That you might bring her to me in some glorious way
Will you please ask God to send her to me very soon
That I may enjoy her love under the full harvest moon

The story behind the poem: It seems that it is God's wish that we forgive all others their transgressions. If we refuse to, He won't forgive our transgressions against Him either.

The Debt

A king's servant owed 10,000 Talents he couldn't possible pay
The lord commanded he be sold into slavery that very day
Servant fell down saying: "Have patience and I will repay all"
The lord, moved by compassion, forgave the debt, didn't stall

The same servant found a fellow servant, owed him 100 pence
Laid on hands, took him by the throat saying: "Pay me hence"
Servant fell down saying: "Have patience and I will repay all"
He would not: cast him into prison for many a long fall

The king heard about this and said: "O thou wicked servant"
"I forgave thy vast debt you should have compassion fervent"
The king was angry and delivered him to the torturers to pay
All that was due him for how he acted that same day

"Likewise My heavenly Father will do unto you, as well,
If in your heart forgive not their trespasses, and on it dwell"
The Lord is very clear about this, seems like it to me
We need to forgive those who transgress, don't you see!

The story behind the poem: I told Robin I wanted to email her a poem and asked her for her email address. She said it was "Seven Blessed Angels." My jaw dropped. She said what is wrong? I said "You are the one." I didn't explain it to her at the time, but this poem will.

Who We Love

The power to love is held in my hands
I control my destiny while on this land
The right to choose belongs with us all
Though God suggests for whom we fall

As always we are allowed to look away
Choose a different path, though we stray
I have my own trinity to lead me there
Heart, soul and mind and a lot of prayer

You were sent to me that I might choose
And find a way for your heart to infuse
I control not the feelings in your heart
You must find love from the very start

No longer in control, my heart has decided
You are "the one"; my soul is so excited
Now I must wait; reveal it to you on queue
That the love of your life is waiting for you

The story behind the poem: "Happy" asked me to write her a poem about the gifts we have. After it was done, I liked it so well I made 40 copies, put them in 5" x 7" frames and gave them out to friends as Christmas presents. They were well received.

Gifts of God

We all have a special gift. both you and me
Given to us by God so everyone might see
It's up to us to find out what that gift is
And learn how we should use it. the will is His

Some people are very psychic. know you well
And their insight uncanny. of visions they tell
Then there is the artist with brush and paint
Creates a landscape with the soul of a saint

Fisherman there are abounding in our midst
Catching wayward souls to be added to the list
The rewards are great for the catch of the day
A lost soul for God returned come what may

The poet is but a dreamer who plays with words
Touches your heart then flies away like a bird
He can reveal your soul. makes you see yourself
His job done. puts his heart back on the shelf

The story behind the poem: Robin asked me to write her a poem about her father, who was deceased, and her sisters. The twins, Robin and "Happy," are the youngest of seven daughters their father had. He always called them his "Seven Blessed Angels."

Seven Blessed Angels

Seven Blessed Angels God gave to me
And a loving wife who brought them to be
How fortunate I am to be loved like this
In heaven knowing eight angels I kissed

I am gone now, but I will always be there
My love for you I feel honored to share
Joy you brought my life as never before
It was heaven on earth, my heart soars

I can not wait until you are here with me
So that you may know God and eternity
Find your soul; don't dare let it get away
Will need that ticket to find me someday

Now it is your turn to find your true love
That melts your soul, places you above
You will know him, 'cuz his heart is pure
And his love for you will forever endure

The story behind the poem: My mother died sometime back. I have been wishing I had treated her differently while she was alive.

Mother

Mother went to heaven, been several years now
Raised five sons, by herself, but I don't know how
Didn't go to see her much for the last few years
She didn't know who I was and that brought tears

Should have gone there anyway, that I now know
Out of love and respect for her that I should show
Now I have no more chance for her love to share
To show her how I feel, and how much I care

A lesson you should really learn from all of this
Give mother love and respect, 'cuz you will miss
You had better do it right now, while you still can
Figure out the best way and put it into your plans

Your mother brought you into this world we know
Gave you discipline, a home and love she showed
Least you can do, make her last days a pleasure
Because the time spent with her you will treasure

The story behind the poem: This poem was inspired by the gospel according to Mark. I liked it the first time I read it and decided to use it in this book.

John The Baptist

John baptized in the wild, preaching repentance of sins
Clothed with camel hair, and his loins girdled with skins
He spoke with the voice of one crying in the wild:
"Make straight the path of the Lord: come to Him as a child"

"There comes one mightier than I, after me," he said
"That I am not worthy to unloose His sandals for bed"
"I baptize with water: He baptizes with the Holy Ghost
That your sins might be forgiven: join the heavenly host"

Jesus came from Nazareth out of Galilee, it would seem
To be baptized by John in the Jordan River, as God deems
Upon coming out of the water the heavens opened up wide
The Holy Spirit descended on Him as a dove in a glide

Then a voice came from heaven, from the one God above
Speaking to those that were gathered, sharing their love
And also to Jesus, that His thoughts would be appeased
"Thou art my beloved Son, in whom I am well pleased"

The story behind the poem: When I first wrote this poem it did not have a title. I simply wrote "love" vertically on the paper. This is how it came out. Now the title is clear.

Love

Long ago and far away my heart was lost
Now I must find it again, whatever the cost
You have shown me the way a friend can be
Pieced me back together that I might be me

Overwhelming emotions you kindle inside
They came to life when your name I abide
My life was but over when you came along
See pure and white and your aura is strong

Voices there are that sing and call your name
You are like no other, no one is the same
I just want to love you, and hope it's allowed
My heart is not stone, feelings are endowed

Eternally thankful for you I will always be
For showing me the way to my true destiny
What is in store for us is impossible to tell
But life without you in it would be like hell

The story behind the poem: I met a lady recently that said: "Mexico has taken over our town without firing a shot." I felt the discrimination in those words and decided to address it in this poem.

Love Knows No Color

Whether your skin is red, black, white or brown
Is of no concern, you are welcome in my town
Love knows no color 'cause we're all one inside
Whoever you are, you should be filled with pride

And what color is our God, some of you may ask?
He will remain invisible until we complete our task
Love is invisible too, at least that is what they say
But see it expressed and received every single day

How can you see something that isn't even there?
All you have to do, open your heart and really care
Pray to God that when the Judgment time arrives
You will only be judged for what you did while alive

To love one another was all He asked us to do
He set an example to be followed by me and you
God loves us all equally, and I am sure He does
So why can't we look beyond color, and just love?

The story behind the poem: I had been thinking about how to project myself. The result: Tell it like it is. Some will like it, some won't.

Who We Are

It's better to be hated for that which you are
Than to be loved for who you aren't, by far
To show one's true self in this game of life
Should be your goal so to avoid all the strife

When you show them who you really truly are
Your soul mate can find you, from near or far
If you play the fool's game of deceiving them
You will find your heart you will often mend

How can you expect to find that one true love
That adores you totally and places you above
If the you, you present are not really there?
How do you expect this person's love to share?

You need to be totally honest, this I'm very sure
To be able to find true love that forever endures
Tell it like it really is, it's the only reasonable way
To avoid heartache you will surely find someday

The story behind the poem: I wrote a poem similar to this to a woman I knew. Later I realized that I was the one with the wall, not her, so I rewrote it to fit my own situation.

The Wall

I built a wall around my heart many years ago
To protect it, leaving only room for blood to flow
That has served me well for all these past years
It saved me from a lot of grief and even tears

Love can't penetrate a wall built such as this
Many have tried and failed, fallen into the abyss
Then you called to me and again I turned away
"Don't even go there" I could hear my heart say

Then you tore down my very carefully built wall
One little brick at a time, and watched it fall
Now my defenses are scattered all over the place
Not standing a chance when I look into your face

Now my heart is very naked, and seeking a cure
Wants to be filled with love that forever endures
You have destroyed my brick wall, it is no more
Now it's all up to you my own heart to restore

The story behind the poem: I have known several people over the years that were "height impaired." It didn't effect their work, or strangely, their attitude either. God bless them.

"Little" People

There's no such thing as "little" people: just small of stature
Need to understand how they feel: heart is just in rapture
Their height has nothing to do with the size of their heart
Heart can be as big as outdoors: usually is for a start

What they do for a living just doesn't matter much either
As long as it's useful and honest and provides leisure
The only thing "little" about them. the size of their body
Rarely find one of them that does work that is shoddy

You think of them as handicapped. but they really aren't
Very good minds come in small packages just for a start
They can do most everything you and I do. only better
Not hampered by their size. just do it by the letter

When it comes to salvation do you think God really cares
What size their body is, or if people on the street stare?
Fortunately their soul doesn't take up much room at all
But. a clean one gets them to heaven. just like those tall

The story behind the poem: Got to thinking of those poor souls on those chain gangs of the past. Life was rough and hopeless. Do your time or die, those were the options.

One More Mile

I am my own worst enemy, you can be certain of that
Can tell by these black and white stripes on my back
My only job: using a hammer to turn rocks into stones
All I get for my trouble: hurting body and aching bones

Been here forty long years, not at all young any more
Wasted my life on this chain gang of blood and gore
When I get out of this place not going to look back
Will leave it all far behind me and that's a true fact

Weary body and mind have all but driven me insane
But my time here is about up: my sanity still remains
They said was all up to me to try and make amends
It was here I found God: to my troubles He will tend

One more mile to pay atonement for my honor less past
One more mile to reach my heavenly Father at last
Now after all these years I have something to show
For many miles behind me: one more mile to go

The story behind the poem: I am sure we have all had dreams that seemed so real. That's the way this one was.

Ghost Riders

Had a very wild, real dream not so many nights ago
About driving a herd to Tucson; tough row to hoe
We were heading out from Amarillo, many miles ahead
Just prayed to God would make it lest we all got dead

Twelve hundred head with thirteen cowboys and a cook
Some old timers and a handful of teenage boys it took
Still two hundred miles to go on a very clear, dark night
Cocked, loaded and ready, could be trouble 'fore daylight

My turn for long night riding, dang, can't even hum a tune
Cows are getting restless, and here comes the full moon
Then I see them silhouetted on a hilltop off to the right
Twenty Indians, maybe more, and they're itching for a fight

The one with all those feathers is riding a big black stud
Breathing fire out his nostrils with steel hooves in the mud
Knew we were in trouble 'cuz they have Winchesters too
Crack! Bullets zinging by where my hair once grew

Just to save our hides, cut them out a few extra head
A peace offering if you would; the braves got well fed
Always a good idea to start out with a few extra beeves
Then woke up before it was over; one of my pet peeves

The story behind the poem: I got the chance to talk to Robin for about an hour today. It was a very enjoyable experience, even though the opportunities are far apart. Of course she inspired this poem. Isn't that always the case?

Aura

There is an aura about her that her beauty can't hide
I see it when I enter the room, stand by her side
The aura is more beautiful than even that of her face
Because it comes from inside, makes my heart race

How can she do all these things to me that she does?
Without saying a word, quiet as an angel from above
You would think by now would be old enough to know
That a woman like her would touch my very inner soul

Fell in love with her, in spite of the others, you see?
There was the husband, the boyfriend and then me
She loves me as a friend, at least I know that much
Every once in a while even get to feel her soft touch

Hugs and kiss on the cheek, enough to last a year
Just have to know that she is around ever so near
My secret dream, will admit, that could come true
That she is dreaming all night about loving me too

The Story behind the poem: When the stories of mass destruction by Katrina and Rita hit the airwaves, it brought on this poem. People need to understand that the loss of worldly possessions is not nearly as important as the loss of their soul.

Storms

What if, in the middle of the night, a meteor should hit?
Huge fireball from the sky, and the very heavens it lit
Caused mass destruction to at least half of the earth
Life would end as it is now, it would cause a rebirth

Loss of homes, possessions, family and such things
Are cause to make you more humble, praises to sing
Your very life was spared, you have a second chance
Give your soul back to God, your eternity it will enhance

Houses, boats and Blue Chips don't mean a thing at all
Were you to give up your soul and take that eternal fall
Have been down that road at least several times before
Speak from experience, He's shown me the open door

There is always some good to come out of these things
It's God's wake up call to you, your ears it should ring
Adversity is a part of life, should learn to handle it well
'Cuz if you don't get it right, could spend eternity in hell

The story behind the poem: This one was inspired by a friend that said we must turn our lives over to God. It just flowed.

The Plow

There once was an old farmer out plowing the back forty
Behind a couple of aged mules named Tuck and Shorty
He was plowing very deep, turning over the black soil
The day was hot and humid, for many hours he toiled

He watched as the ground rose up and then turned over
Exposing the new earth to the sun to grow some clover
As he walked behind the mules a loud "clang" rang out
Mules stopped in their tracks, couldn't move it no doubt

The farmer began digging to find out what it was he hit
Discovered a two foot tall urn, brass, an inscription on it
It read: "He turned water into wine, made the blind see
Turn your life over to Him; enjoy heaven for all eternity"

The farmer took home the urn and pondered it for awhile
The words rang in his ears, to his face brought a smile
Then and there made a commitment to be one with God
Turned over his heart to Jesus, more important than sod

The story behind the poem: I went for a walk and my knees were hurting. That brought on this poem.

Kneeling Down

Kneeling down is a very painful thing for me to do
Had a bad injury years ago, and tore ligaments too
When I kneel to say prayers the pain is intense
So, I think of Him with nails in His hands; immense!

The pain He suffered would be unbearable to most
The pain I suffer, nothing of which I can boast
I just put up with it the best way that I can
Try to think of Him and those nails in His hands

Your real perspective in this life should always be
There are always those who are worse off than me
Count your blessings, of these you have a full store
Pray to God and He might just give you some more

Your heart, soul and mind is where it really counts
Give them all to God right down to the last ounce
All of your worldly goods matter so very, very little
Eternity is the prize, unless you choose to belittle

The story behind the poem: I was to meet her again on the next day. She had "grabbed" my attention with the things she said, and her obvious love of God and her fellow man.

Counting The Hours

Counting the hours until we meet again, at long last
We will discuss the future, as well as the short past
You have the heart, soul and mind I am looking for
Don't need to project in you what your mind stores

You have triggered my memory; of you I have some
But, when I think of you maybe you are "the one"
You're so very comfortable in my mind, so it seems
Maybe you're "the one" I have had in my dreams?

So how can it be that this should come at long last?
Are my sins forgiven for all the wrongs in my past?
All that I can now see is the future with you in there
Loving me and showing me just how much you care

Only time will tell, as things such as these surely do
To see if something really becomes of me and you
Your heart is ever so pure and your mind unspoiled
And the ground you walk on will be forever unsoiled

The story behind the poem: This happened to me this morning about 5:30 A.M. It made my day.

Kindness

Met a Mexican one morning, he had just got out of jail
He needed to get home fast, to California, without fail
Had a check for a hundred from Prisoner's Trust Fund
And needed to cash it so he could make his bus run

Drove him all around town, at least four or five places
No one would cash his check, didn't know of our faces
Greyhound bus was going to leave, half an hour, or so
Was getting very desperate, what if everyone said no?

Reached deep into my pocket, found a hundred bucks
Gave it to him, told him he had a change of luck
Made his bus just in time, was very thankful you know
Waved goodbye as it pulled away, his gratitude to show

To help when able, is the lesson you're to learn here
It will all come back ten-fold, because life is a mirror
To reach out and touch someone is not just a saying
Should become a way of life, just like that of praying

The story behind the poem: I couldn't help but notice that a lot of people seem to confuse knowledge with wisdom. Maybe this will help.

Wisdom

Knowledge and wisdom, not even close to the same thing
Knowledge will make a living; wisdom, a full life it will bring
Wisdom comes from the ability to be still and not think
Brings out the real you; heart, soul and mind it will link

Power without wisdom is a very dangerous thing at best
Seems someone is always wanting to put it to the test
Can you imagine an all powerful God without wisdom inside?
Chaos would reign over the universe and this earth we abide

Computers hold vast amounts of knowledge, that's for sure
But without the wisdom of man, just machines that endure
A computer has no compassion, judgment, or even love
Simply follows the directions given by the programmer above

If you want to give your heart away where it really counts
Give it to Him who has all wisdom, knowledge and life's fount
There is a place waiting for you, and those of yours
Ask God to reserve you a spot, while you finish your chores

The story behind the poem: I was taking a break from writing when this poem just flooded my mind. I had butterflies the whole time I was writing it and my hands were shaking as well. I could "feel" The Spirit in me. I was truly inspired when I wrote this version of the crucifixion.

The Tree of Forgiveness

I am the famous tree that was hewn into His cross
The one He hung from to show hope was not lost
It was an honor that they should have chosen me
To hold Him up there that all the world might see

I am the thorns with which they crowned His head
Cut from the brambles to prove that which He said
He was a King, no doubt, there for everyone to see
I became the one to prove it to both you and me

I am the big iron nails used to pierce his soft flesh
Drove me deep into the cross; our matter to mesh
To hold Him up there it was commanded that I do
So He might offer God's forgiveness to me and you

I am the long, slender lance used to pierce His side
To prove He was dead they shoved me deep inside
Now I don't feel so bad in this new life anymore
Knowing that He was resurrected to open the door

The story behind the poem: Peace is something we all want and desire. You need to realize that all true peace begins within.

P.E.A.C.E.
(Praying Every Afternoon Changes Everyone)

When you pray for someone, it will change you too
The good things you ask for them might come true
The changes you see in them might be so very little
But, the changes in yourself puts you in the middle

When you place yourself between them and God
You act as their shield, that He might spare the rod
You are the beacon of light they are looking for
Shining down from heaven, showing thru every pore

To pray for others is a very good and worthy calling
So, why not get started now and quit your stalling?
The worst that can happen is you get closer to God
And for your efforts to Him, He will give you a nod

"Ask and you shall receive," was from Him that said
You should always pray to Him before you go to bed
Some of the best gifts that God has ever given by far
Are unanswered prayers, 'cuz He knows who you are

The story behind the poem: A lot of people think all they have to do to get to heaven is believe that Jesus Christ is the Son of God and they will be saved. But, even the demons in hell believe in God. Believing is not enough. It takes faith, love, obedience and works to make the cut.

Faith

Jesus then said: "According to your faith be it unto you."
The lepers were cleansed, and blind made to see too
The lame made to walk without any crutches from birth
He healed most everyone, from every part of this earth

They all had one thing in common, that's for sure
An unshakable faith in Him and His ability to cure
Without that faith Jesus would not have gone ahead
And made them whole from their feet to their head

It's not a blind faith He's asking us to believe here
But based on The Word of God spoken loud and clear
Faith can move a mountain, He has promised us that
Just have to have faith in Him and that's a true fact

Faith without works serves very little purpose, I'm told
Must show God your love by obeying the laws He holds
Acts you do express love more than anything you say
Why don't you be one with God and do it His way?

The story behind the poem: I was sitting here writing when this thought just came to me. I think God is speaking to me as well, I just write the words down.

The Hammer and The Anvil

God is The Big Hammer, and the anvil is your life
He is there to shape you, and add a little spice
Have you ever noticed that when things go wrong
There is a ringing in your ears playing your song?

He is talking to you and giving you that wake-up call
You had better listen to Him, lest you take the big fall
You can ignore it if you wish and then pay the price
Up to you, take a chance with the roll of the dice

If you don't want to gamble and play the sure thing
God is the answer, get to heaven, His praises sing
He has big plans for you when you arrive up there
With love, happiness and eternity He wants to share

So when you are caught in a trap and have no outs
Lift a loud voice to Heaven and let out a big shout
He will listen carefully to you, because that is His way
The Hammer will strike the anvil and make a new day

The story behind the poem: I was thinking about the women I had loved in my lifetime. Now I had finally found the one that was all of the good things I had experienced with all of them.

Love You

More than all the women that I ever loved
More than the sum of the parts of all above
How can it be, you should be as total as this
To fill my heart with love, my soul with bliss?

You have honored my presence by being there
My soul you elevate by love, showing you care
Your acts of service to me very special indeed
You anticipate and fill my every want and need

I long to touch you, with me a very major prize
It's not yet allowed, your emotions it would rise
My time is close at hand, I am so sure of that
To show you what real love is and where it's at

Will patiently wait until your heart needs filling
Show you what real love is, if you are willing
Just need a chance to show how much I care
So maybe you and me will have a life to share

The story behind the poem: People need to realize that you can pray anywhere; while working, playing, driving or doing most anything.

Churches

A church is not the only place to pray, you see
I don't need one to talk to God, as it should be
To worship Him in spirit and truth we were asked
So that prayers sent to Him would eternally last

His Son came to pave the way for you and me
We just have to follow His rules, don't you see?
We are forgiven for all the bad things that we do
Suffered the cross, gave a chance to me and you

He sent His only son, what more could we ask?
Gave a chance at heaven, be thankful it will last
The rewards are great for obeying all of the rules
Overlooks our misdeeds while giving us the tools

Heaven is love and forgiveness at its very best
All we have to do to get there is pass the test
Would think all of the rewards would be sufficient
To provide the real incentives to make us efficient

The story behind the poem: Last night I would get a nice review of my book from an RN that said she had a family member that was bi-polar, and wasn't doing very well with it. I was inspired to write the "family member" this poem the next morning to try and help.

P.U.S.H.

Purposes in this life are never very easily known
One thing is certain, will reap that which is sown
The "rock" that God gave you in this life of yours
Is for you to push against until the blood pours

Until you've released every bit of effort you have
You must keep trying, your wounds He will salve
To put forth with your best effort, all that He asks
One of His ways of letting us make up for the past

Surely you should know your character it will build
By overcoming the trials of your life that He filled
He didn't say you had to move it, that's His will
He just asked us to but try, until our energy is nil

He says we should push, then push some more
It will change your being down to the very core
"Pray Until Something Happens," He asks we do
That He may show love endures for me and you

The story behind the poem: On Valentines Day I would give Robin a bouquet of beautiful flowers. Just being a friend, of course.

A Friend

Roses they are not, but might should be
To express the things that you do to me
I must be careful and not get out of line
This is not the right place, nor right time

I know you are hurting, I feel it from here
But your heart and mind should show no fear
Your life is in front of you, not in your past
And you will find love that will forever last

Just so you know, I'm someone who cares
And with your burden I am willing to share
Have a big shoulder when you need to cry
And look into your soul through your eyes

Wish Valentines Day hope that all goes fine
With your new home and your life this time
When you desire anything, anything at all
You have a friend, all you need to do is call

The story behind the poem: I picked up a woman in my cab one day from a motel. I knew her as a bartender. She was very sad and told me her grandfather had just died the hour before. I had just written this poem the night before and read it to her. It caused many tears. I told her it was her grandfather speaking to her.

Angel Wings

Do you think God could use another angel, maybe even me?
I would requisition for beautiful wings, large ones, you see?
Then I would fly about; look down on the earth far below
If God would allow it, I'd go there, my love to show

Would rest on your shoulder, wouldn't even know I'm there
Until the sun shown behind, at my shadow you would stare
I'll be right there with you, there is never cause for alarm
Will look forever after you, so to you there comes no harm

I'll ask God for that to be my duty this heavenly life
Spend it with you forever, and eliminate your earthly strife
Then I will know what this heaven really does mean to me
Can look up and see God; back on earth with you be

Now I know how it is to experience heaven on this earth
Just have to die first, then give my own soul a rebirth
If that's the only single way I can be forever with you
Then Jesus please take me now, so I'll be with You too

The story behind the poem: I had a dream, and there she was, standing in front of me. It took my breath away.

The Woman in My Dreams

Her heart is pure and her mind is ever so clear
All I will ever ask is that she remain so very near
I have only known her but for a very short while
But think her and me can go that legendary mile

We need to go slowly, find out what matters most
Find a reason to be together with God as our host
Already in love with her; she must learn to love me
See the faults in each other, whatever they can be

Real true love; the only choice, so very sure of that
It surpasses all the bells and whistles, that is a fact
It will last for an eternity until to heaven we both go
It comes only once in a lifetime, this you surely know

Can't say it will be that easy, these things never are
Then, never easy either, to hang your hat on a star
If you desire to win in life's game as you get older
Must give your heart away, take a chance, be bolder

The story behind the poem: Everyone has the same question. Why am I here? The answer is simple. You are a child of God. He asks us to surrender totally to Him and in exchange He will save our souls and take us to heaven with Him. That's the best deal you will ever get.

A Purpose Driven Life

A purpose driven life is what you should want to achieve
A life driven by God's Word, that surely won't deceive
You get out of life what you put into it, it has been said
Most of that has to do with what you put into your head

GI-GO in computer talk means garbage in, garbage out
Your mind gives you what you feed it, this there's no doubt
If you want to be a better Christian, The Word is the way
Study the Bible every day to find out what God has to say

Answers to daily problems, challenges, goals and the like
Can all be found in the Bible, tell the devil to take a hike
It is the greatest book written, the greatest story ever told
Written by the hand of God to bring you into His fold

So if your goal is to get to heaven, and I surely hope it is
Give to Caesar what is Caesars, and to God what is His
You can't earn heaven, you can only get there by grace
Given to you by God, and the devil in you He will replace

The story behind the poem: I met someone who was talking of the friends we all have, some affect us well, some don't. It is wise to pick your friends carefully.

Friends We Choose

With friends you choose you should be careful indeed
Because their advice you are the most likely to heed
Advice too freely given, not always that which is good
Tells you what you shouldn't do, and what you should

The best guide by far is your own innermost spirit
Tells you what you should do, your best interest in it
This advice is for you, comes from your heart and soul
It will govern your being and lay rest to your foes

The quality of any person, you can always surely tell
By the quality of those chosen to call friends as well
Your friends are an extension of your very own being
Their caring and love; what you in yourself are seeing

We all need many friends, of this I am very sure
Without them in it, life would go by in a blur
Choose wisely, they will make a difference in your fate
The best friend you will ever have should be your mate

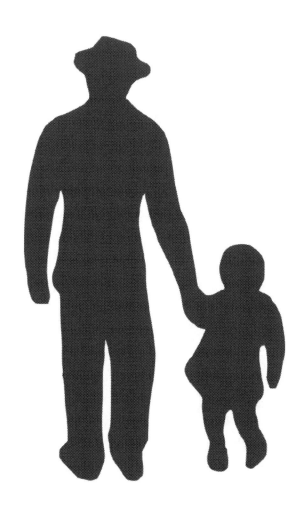

The story behind the poem: My father died when I was about two years old. I never really knew him but have often wondered how it must be to have a father. Later in life, I came to know what a father's love was through the love I saw in my father-in-law, Lee. I dedicate this poem to him.

Love Thy Father

The tears ran down the face of the man in the chair
He just learned he had cancer, the news he must share
He didn't have any insurance and money was very tight
He couldn't afford the treatments that might save his life

His five-year old son entered the room and saw him crying
Grabbed a hankie and his daddy's tears he started drying
The young boy then said: "Whatever has happened to you?"
"Daddys aren't supposed to cry, what made you so blue?"

With that the big man explained the situation to his only son
That he may not be around much longer, to play and run
The young boy left, his very heart broken, and in tears too
He went upstairs to his room to decide what he should do

Daddy had said: "Time takes money", and it rang in his ear
What could he do for his daddy that would keep him near?
Broke open his piggy bank, said, with money in his grasp:
"How much time can I buy for $27.42, will it forever last?"

The story behind the poem: Robin said: "A penny for your thoughts." I told her not today, I would tell her in a poem the next day. The next day I saw Robin, with sister "Happy", and asked her for a penny. She gave it to me, and I gave her this poem.

Lone Wolf

When will true love come to a man such as I?
I am like a lone wolf in the woods who cries
He pines for his mate with a howl that hurts
Spreading his soul to the wind, feet in the dirt

He thinks he has found her, but is unsure
She's moving very fast and her heart is a blur
If she would but slow down, the roses to smell
Then he could see her heart that he might tell

He has made his intentions clear to perfection
All she has to do is see herself in the reflection
He just wants her close by, so very, very near
So, someday home she will come, mind clear

His soul cries out over the wind driven snow
Howling out her name, so very soft and low
When will it begin, that one true love that lasts
That forever binds, under God, in stone cast?

The story behind the poem: A hike through the woods one day revealed a berry bush. I was hungry but had heard that some berries were poisonous so declined to try them. You should not take a chance with your life...or your soul.

The Arborist

A tree, or person, bears fruit only after its own kind
This is all according to the plan that's in God's mind
The cause is not the fruit, but the nature of the tree
Trees with inedible fruit can't bear good fruit, you see?

You can always identify a person by the fruit produced
Can't expect him to gain heaven by girls he's seduced
You can always tell a genuine Christian by his deeds
Not by how religious he is, or by prayer that he leads

How you choose to live is really what it's all about
Trees growing bad fruit, cut down and burned, no doubt
Those bearing good fruit through the works they do
Will earn a place in heaven and God's forgiveness too

The only way out for those of us that are here
Is to accept Jesus as our Savior, and hold Him dear
He suffered the cross just to take our sins away
Couldn't do that for ourselves, there just wasn't any way

The story behind the poem: One night Robin asked me to write her a poem about "peace of mind." She had been talking to me about a kitten she had that she loved to hold. That is what inspired the first verse of this poem I wrote for her.

Peace of Mind

A very soft kitten curled up on top your breast
Laying down her little head that she may rest
Paws are stretched out, up around your neck
Inviting you to love her, and yes, you may pet

A place like no other you just have to see
Mill Creek Falls is such a wonderful place to be
The creek cascades into the Rogue, far below
Eases your mind as you're touched by a rainbow

Lithia Park serenity will calm your soul and mind
Rest beside the creek, let your thoughts unwind
Leave your troubles there 'cause I know it works
Empty them from your mind wherever they lurk

Someone to love you as much as you love him
That lasts from now to forever, until the very end
These the things that peace of mind is made of
They will rest your soul, prepare it for Him above

The story behind the poem: I have been getting hungry lately. After a while I realized that it was not for food, it was for some spiritual satisfaction, so I "gave" myself away.

A Full Belly

What good is a full belly with an empty heart?
You need to turn yourself inside out for a start
Those pains in your stomach, not for food to shove
It's your heart crying big tears for the lack of love

We all have that good inside us that's stored within
Happiness is getting it out, wonder where it's been?
Try giving some of yourself, it's the best thing to do
Will find that love given always comes back to you

You can feed your face like there isn't any tomorrow
But is your heart that needs feeding so not to sorrow
Real love given to friends or others that are in need
Like the great tree of life, you're just planting a seed

He said if you give it, it would be given unto you
That which goes around comes around, isn't that true?
Just open your heart and let the good inside flow out
Then lift your voice to heaven, let out a loud shout

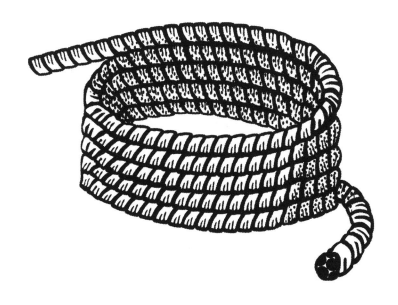

The story behind the poem: This story teaches to not doubt God's Word. When He speaks we should listen.

The Rope

A mountain climber decided to make a big climb at night
He would go it all alone, even though there was no light
Sky was overcast, no stars or moon with which to see
He was trying to get to the top: claim a great victory

He was almost to the top, his foot slipped and he fell
Falling down very fast, it seemed, into the very pits of hell
His life flashed before him, all of the good, and those lies
Screamed out for God to help him, pleading with his cries

All at once the rope around his waist got taunt and held
His descent ended by the tight rope, his hands to it weld
He was dangling in black space, no handholds in sight
Again asked God to save him, praying against the night

The deep voice of God shattered the still, black night too
He said: "What is it you would have Me do for you?"
"Save my life Dear Lord, I will change my ways, I swear"
God said: "Then cut the rope around your waist you wear"

The climber decided to hold tight, without cutting the rope
Although he was cold, because he hadn't brought a coat
The next day searchers found him, frozen solid and dead
Ten feet above safe ground, not heeding what God said

The story behind the poem: I have been single for many years. I have been waiting for "the one". Won't settle for anything less.

Real Love

Have you never really loved at all, never known what it is?
Nothing to do with sex, but in how you choose to live
Your mate becomes the main focal point, without any strife
You love God the most, and then your special mate for life

But it doesn't even end there is eternity that you are making
True love has no end, only a lifetime to keep it from breaking
What you do here on earth just practice for the long haul
Then you can spend eternity loving your God, angels on call

Doesn't that sound like something that you would like to do?
Spend years of joy on earth, get to go to heaven too?
Just need to follow your true dream, it will lead you there
God knows your needs, will find a partner for you to share

Just trust in Him, there is someone special for each of us
Sometimes it takes years but don't settle, or make any fuss
Just follow your dreams, God has given them to you, it seems
That you might fulfill them, and He will give you the means

The story behind the poem: I overheard a conversation and knowing the participants, this poem came to mind.

Honesty

"Honesty is always the best policy." I heard them say
Then cheat on their taxes and their wife along the way
They call in sick to work every day they think they can
Do poor work on the job thinking about that new van

When you lie and cheat others you will pay the price
If not now, then you surely will, in the everlasting life
Lying will sour the soul, your hardened heart gets bolder
That kink in your neck, from looking over your shoulder

Don't you think it's about time for a new start in life?
Live at peace with yourself and eliminate all the strife
There is no time like now to get your priorities straight
Just give your heart to Him, do away with all that hate

You can't love God and be anything but totally honest
Then you will be in line for the rewards as He promised
To do the right thing is your only real practical choice
Then when God calls your name you will hear His voice

The story behind the poem: My sons and I used to go fishing at the coast every year. Those were some of the best times ever.

Fishing With My Sons

My four sons used to really like to go fishing with me
We would rent a big charter boat and head out to sea
When the salmon were biting well, made for a good trip
Chinooks and Silvers, I'd better hold on tight to the grip

The captain would bait our hooks most of the time
He was very, very good at it, and didn't seem to mind
We had loads of fun and filled up our gunny sacks
The captain headed her in, oh no, there's some I lack

Went bottom fishing for perch, snapper and ling cod too
Caught a whole bunch, two or three at a time would do
They make real fine eating when we fillet them just right
Grill them on a Bar-B-Q, with onions, they're out of sight

On the jetty I caught a skate; was four foot six long
Took the bait, headed out to sea, thought he was gone
Finally reeled him in, after a very long battle it seemed
Now could eat well, and pretend to be a man of means

The story behind the poem: I think cowboys have a little bit different mentality than everyone else. It is simple, laid back and concise. By living close to nature they are generally close to God.

The Cowboy in Me

Get up before dawn so the rising sun I might view
Watch God in all His glory light up the orb in hues
Put on my jeans and boots and rub my hurt knee
But, I guess that's just the cowboy God put in me

Get that first cup of hot black Java, that's the best
You can have your coffee houses and all the rest
Say my prayers to Him above, am in need you see
But, I guess that's just the cowboy God put in me

With my poetry and rhymes I could use some help
Women have always inspired me by that which I felt
They provide me with that feeling of sheer ecstasy
But, I guess that's just the cowboy God put in me

The woman needed in my life is nowhere to be seen
Seems God has other plans for me that He deemed
When she does show up, she will probably drink tea
But, I guess that's just the cowboy God put in me

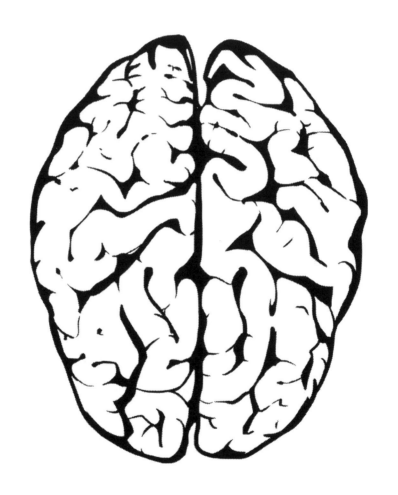

The story behind the poem: Exercising your mind is very important. Who you choose to exercise it with is even more important. Learn to be a leader.

Minds

Be aware of the minds of those that are around you
They just might contain pearls of wisdom that are true
They can be of some help when your direction's unclear
With good advice, freely given, so you have no fear

We all have experiences that are different from all others
Learn to share them with one another, we're all brothers
You can learn a little from them, them a little from you
You might make a friend that will for a lifetime be true

Avoid those minds that are laced with alcohol and drugs
Probably just looking for their next "hit," someone to mug
Their minds are very murky, they can't think straight at all
Punishment handed down by God to pay back for the fall

Choose the minds carefully where you spend your time
They will enhance your own, you'll find friends that bind
Other than your soul, your mind the greatest gift of God
Protect it at all costs until you're buried in the cold sod

The story behind the poem: A friend sent me an email about natural highs. I gleaned this poem from it. There is that different perspective again.

Natural Highs

A natural high, it seems, always the very best kind to have
Try some of these on for size, your wounds it will salve
A special glance, given or received, to one you have not met
Having someone say you're beautiful, hasn't even begun yet

Midnight phone calls that lasts for hours, until morning's light
Talking about holding hands on the beach, of a beautiful sight
Laughing with each other, about nothing, about what you miss
Remembering those goodnight hugs, still feeling that first kiss

Lying in a warm bed, listening to rain gently falling 'til five
Just saying thank you to God that you are very much alive
Falling into love has to be the best experience it would seem
Especially when it's the one that you see in your dreams

Knowing that someone misses you, a blessing itself, for sure
Makes for very sweet dreams, of this you must really concur
So get on out there and make someone's dream come true
It might very well be your own dream returning again to you

The story behind the poem: I had a beautiful mare named "Misty." She was hard to handle, but it was a joy to ride her.

"Misty"

Reared up as she saw it, back feet firmly on the ground
Then dropped her jaw to the earth, never made a sound
Was bred from a Quarter horse, pure Arabian in the mix
Snakes bothered her a lot, even though were really sticks

Coal black, three white socks, a beauty without a doubt
With her neck arched like a bow, tail stuck straight out
Didn't know how to walk, pranced everywhere she went
So concerned with looking pretty her energy she spent

Had to round up my cows; across the creek on far side
"Misty" didn't like water either, this she would not abide
Refused to ford the creek; I couldn't coax her to cross
Had on my new Tony Lama boots; would not be a loss

Ground-reined her, and gently slipped out of the saddle
Grabbed the reins and said: "I need your head to rattle."
Coiled up a big round-house blow, hit her hard as I could
Dropped right to her knees, a sad apology if you would

Got back on, crossed the creek, was calm as could be
Didn't think I was a horse trainer, but that would be me
Just had to get her full attention, works well every time
Now crosses the creek without a complaint on her mind

The story behind the poem: When Robin's stepfather died she told me about it. I wrote this: "Robin, When you told me about Papa Elmer last night I could feel the pain, sorrow and love you feel for him. I tried to capture your feelings for him in this poem. I hope I got close."

Papa Elmer

You have always been a very real father to me
One that you were never. ever. required to be
You took care of me in my many times of need
And your wisdom always there for me to heed

Now that you are forever gone from this sphere
My soul cries out and wishes you were near
My very best friend has now gone to heaven
And his very own daughters really number seven

What a difference we make when we are here
When we show our love for those near and dear
We are only allowed but a very short time to bind
That we might enjoy heaven for a long. long time

I will miss you forever. until I'm there with you
But in the meantime I must find love that is true
You have shown me the way a dear friend can be
Became a true soul mate that will last for eternity

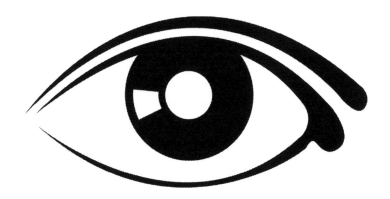

The story behind the poem: A young lady came in and she was obviously very sad. I got her a copy of "She Cries Inside" and read it to her. The tears flowed, and flowed. As it turns out her father drowned the day before. I wrote this for her and she read it at her father's funeral. There was not a dry eye in the house.

Grief

Grief is something that touches your very soul
Much like the sudden death of a newborn foal
Will break your heart into many, many pieces
Into your very own being, and more, it reaches

The tears will flow because that is God's way
Of cleansing the heart making it new someday
The pain will ease because it's just really there
To remind you of a loved one's life you shared

Death has touched me very many times before
A lost son, niece, nephew, what else is in store?
Young life snuffed out, never got a chance to live
Hard to understand His plan, faith we must give

Death is a part of life, of this we surely all know
What matters while we're here: love that we show
We just have to give it, expect nothing in return
It's how a heart grows; that's what I have learned

The story behind the poem: I hadn't seen Robin for some time, but I could still "feel" her touch. When I was thinking about it this poem came to mind.

Your Touch

Your touch excites me and makes my blood flow
Your hug and kiss will even make my heart glow
You send electric charges all through my spine
Don't know how you do this most every time

I can't imagine what a passionate kiss would do
Beyond my comprehension to make love to you
I live in a dream world and you're not really there
So much want to show you how much I care

The stroke of your hand causes my heart to heal
In your touch there is love, and caring that I feel
Feelings, your heart speaking, I know that much
The feelings in your heart are also in your touch

Long to touch you in a very soft and gentle way
Have you touch me, see what hands have to say
I have the magic touch, you will turn to jelly inside
Heart and soul will melt as I take them for a ride

The story behind the poem: I have used many stories in writing this poem book in order to get the message across. Something that I have learned from the Master.

Talents

A talent was a measure of weight used in ancient times
Jesus used it in stories and parables, and I in my rhymes
The servants were given talents that they should multiply
One was given five, another two, the last just one to try

The Master returned and with the first two was very pleased
It seems they doubled their talents. Master was appeased
The third servant did sin: hid his one and only talent away
Had no incentive to invest it, thought he'd do it his way

This bad servant the Master rebuked and severely scold
Took his talent away and gave it to another servant to hold
The story is so very easy to understand, seems to me
We were all given talents; instructions to use them, you see!

If you don't use your God-given talents the way He intended
He will take them away from you, 'cuz your time has ended
You will miss the great reward He has waiting there for you
So, use them in the right way, show God your heart's true

The story behind the poem: Well, it happened again. Another song on the radio that I put a different twist too. I hope you enjoy it.

God's Little Moments

You see that little discolored spot on your upper arm
Think it might be cancer, that could do a lot of harm
You say a little prayer, in a week or two it's gone
God's little moments such as that make you strong

You watch a new foal being born, all slippery and wet
Notice he is not breathing; push hard on his chest
The air enters his lungs and he starts breathing at last
God's little moments like that have made up my past

To see my oldest son take his very first step and fall
He's not quite ready yet, decides he needs to crawl
Grew into a big boy, before he was taken far above
Thank God for those little moments He gave to love

Now I have found the woman that I want for my wife
The one I choose to love for the rest of my life
If He will only help her see the bright, true light
My life would be full of God's little moments all night

The story behind the poem: A friend of mine got a wonderful hug from the girl sitting next to him in church last Sunday. It made his day. When he related the incident to me it brought on this poem. (Hugs can heal what is wrong with you)

Hugs

Giving a hug is a form of showing love, you see?
Always seems to contain a large amount of electricity
When you hug someone your hearts very nearly touch
Why don't you hug a friend you care about much?

You can extend your arm out for a good handshake
Or wrap your arms around them and their day make
The approach you choose tells them how you feel
How glad you are to see them; friendships it will seal

A hug is such a wonderful way to say hello to friends
Even to a stranger; 'round your finger they will bend
When your arms hold on tight, can feel their heartbeat
Embraces your whole body; sweeps you off your feet

Heaven on earth revolves around hugs; makes you purr
God's preferred method of greeting. I am very sure
What's alright with God is surely alright with me
How long should a hug last? Conger the better, you see?

The story behind the poem: A friend sent me an email last night. She said she had three or four bad days in a row. That triggered this poem right then and there.

Getting Down

Some days when you arise it doesn't start off well
It's going to be a very bad day, you can just tell
You need to turn it around the best way you can
Get your head together and come up with a plan

The best way, by far, try and start off with a prayer
Ask for a little bit of help with your troubles to bear
Will set the tone for the day, give you some hope
Make your day easier, with problems you can cope

The prayer isn't even about what God does for you
But the good feeling you get by that which you do
Prayer, a peaceful way to begin your day it seems
Let God in to help so He might fulfill your dreams

It is an attitude thing, this you should surely know
Give respect due God, for Him your love to show
One day at a time, how He said we should get by
All that God will ever ask is that we but try

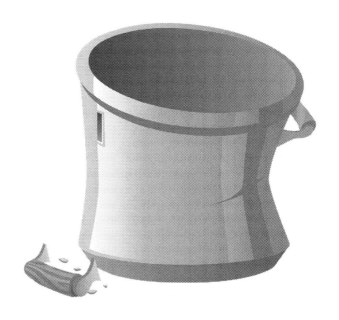

The story behind the poem: I hadn't written anything in over a week and then this thought just came to me one evening, so, I wrote it down.

Love Until You're Empty

Love until you're empty 'cuz you can't give it all away
Will come back to you ten-fold and find a place to stay
The more you try to give it away, and find you can't
The more you will realize that love has a different slant

It's one of the few things in this glorious life we lead
That you can't give away, it's like a boomerang of need
Love costs nothing to give so it's hard to go broke
But love returned, priceless, your very heart it will stoke

Can you think of a monetary investment you could make
That costs very little but would be priceless in its wake?
Were there very many of those, then we would all be rich
Why not try love, play a new song with a different pitch?

Jesus said we should love one another, that was His plea
He loved us all enough to die on the cross, you see?
Not asking you to terminate here, only live a life of love
'Cuz by doing so you will find a place in heaven above

The story behind the poem: She was always all smiles, but she was hurting bad. I could feel it and wanted her to cry so she would feel better. A lot of women have cried to this poem.

She Cries Inside

Her pretty smile will brighten hearts from afar
Her eyes twinkle like they were made of stars
She makes you feel welcome around the fire
They all come to see her and they never tire

You would never guess, not in a thousand years
That she is crying inside with big crocodile tears
She keeps it all inside so no one will know
Her weeping, very silent, and it will never show

This is her way, can't even pretend to know why
She holds it all inside, she's even unable to cry
I wish I could hold her so she could let it drain
Brush the tears from her face to ease her pain

God wishes us to shed a tear, now and then
It eases the pain and your soul it will mend
You just have to show it to someone that cares
Someone that loves you and your pain will bear

The story behind the poem: I saw someone the other day that I had wronged in the past. I had made a decision about his character that I had no right to make. We talked about it and I asked for his forgiveness. He was kind enough to give it to me.

Mending Fences

Every rancher knows there comes time to mend fences
On a farm, in relationships, you can tell by your senses
When you wrong someone, or maybe they wronged you
You need to repair the gap to retain a friend that's true

It's hard to get by without saying, or doing, anything bad
You can tell where you are because it makes them sad
They don't want to lose you, anymore than you do them
Better check your fences, find what you need to mend

That same thing is true for that only woman in your life
She might be just your lover or maybe even your wife
Fences are easy to repair when the damage is slight
Let it get out of hand, you're surely in for a fight

Good friends are hard to come by, as only God knows
Keep the ones you've made, make friendships grow
Admit when you are wrong, it's not always easy to do
Find forgiveness when the wrongs were done to you

The story behind the poem: I have an opinion, of course. Don't we all? However, my opinion is correct. (Hee, hee). I gave a copy of this poem to the most opinionated man I know. He just laughed. (But, he got the point.) Why don't you try it?

Opinions

An opinion: little more than a bundle of thoughts, you see
Taken from your perspective of how things ought to be
These thoughts are then processed in your own mind
As the gospel truth, as you see it, for others to find

The trouble with opinions is just about everybody has one
A cheap commodity, I am sure; with them have some fun
Most opinions are formed without sufficient true facts
Just a feeling about how you think; how you should react

I always laugh when I hear someone say: "In my opinion"
I am about to hear truth distorted by their mind's minion
Politicians are the worst when it comes to dubious facts
Change them daily to fit the situation; the truth we lack

When you speak it's better to know from where truth comes
Than it is to have a weak opinion like most everyone
An opinion is of little use to the sender or receiver
Called just "blowing smoke" by us that are perceivers

The story behind the poem: In a passage from the Bible I read Jesus voices His displeasure about "words without knowledge." I took it from there.

Words Without Knowledge

Words without knowledge seem to be spoken by most
With gossip, idle chatter, even about the heavenly host
If you want to get it right, must go to the source
Read the Bible for yourself; even interpret it, of course

Lots of people have their opinions of theological scope
Having never read the Bible there's very little hope
Don't you always listen to experts about taxes and such?
Should get an educated opinion on what matters much

How can you obey God's laws not knowing what they are?
Ignorance of the law no excuse, not here or there, by far
If you want to do it right must do it for yourself
Buy a Bible for your own and take it off the shelf

The rules are not complicated; have to learn how to love
Love all others, yourself and the only one God above
If you can learn how to love, feel it from the heart
On eternity and heaven you will have a very big start

The story behind the poem: Robin was in a bad accident. I had warned her four months before that this was bound to happen. I was so upset I couldn't write this poem until three weeks after it happened.

Broken Angel

Saw you lying there on that sterile hospital bed
All cut up, broken, bruised and very nearly dead
Your eyes were closed, didn't know I was there
Came to see you and with your pain to share

My heart felt for you seeing your hair in disarray
Wanted you to know I loved you, all I could say
Said a prayer to Saint Jude that you'd be alright
You said: "Please don't go" as I said goodnight

It was an accident they claim, but it was foretold
A warning you were given for your mind to hold
The harm that I saw for you, you chose to ignore
Now it has happened, you are all bloody and sore

It's time for a change in this life you lead
God's hand has touched you, you should heed
A second chance most of us will never get
Make good use of it so you won't live to regret

The story behind the poem: There is a car dealer in my town by the name of Sole Savers. That's what prompted me to write this poem. I have often thought it would be a good name for a shoe repair shop.

Sole Savers Shop

Went to the Sole Savers Shop to get my boots repaired
They were in need of soles and heels, like nobody cared
Got them back in three weeks, were all shiny and new
Of course, it cost me half a hundred, plus a five spot too

Wouldn't it be awesome to be able to re-soul yourself?
Spend a hundred or two and give your soul new health?
Then the road to eternity would be paved in dollar bills
You can buy your way to heaven on an airline with frills

Well, it doesn't work that way, guess it never really did
Can't buy your way to a clean soul, no matter what's bid
Guess what? Now you can get a clean soul for free
Because Jesus loved us enough to hang on that tree

All your sins will be gone just as soon as you commit
Give your heart to Jesus, to His will you should submit
Then your soul will be as white as the wind driven snow
His drops of blood you see are real; not there for show

The story behind the poem: It would seem the punishment for adultery in Biblical times was rather severe. We don't do that anymore, thank God. However, the spiritual penalty is the same now as it was then. But, any sin can be forgiven. "Judge not, and ye shall not be judged."

Adultery

One morning Jesus went to the Mount of Olives to pray
Afterward, He went to the temple to teach law His way
Woman was brought to Him, caught in adultery with a Jew
Pharisees then said: "She must be stoned, what say You?"

Moses' law required her to be stoned outside of town
And Jesus wrote in the dirt like he hadn't heard a sound
They continued to question Him: "Moses' law," they said
"Required that they indeed stone her until she was dead"

Jesus rose up said to the Pharisees, knowing their past:
"He who is without sin among you, the first stone cast"
Convicted by their own conscience, they left in a hurry
Beginning with the oldest, even to the last they scurried

Then He said to the woman: "Where are your accusers?
Has no one condemned you, even Pharisee abusers?"
"No one my Lord", she said, Jesus' love He would pour:
"Neither do I condemn you: go home and sin no more."

The story behind the poem: This is yet another poem that was inspired by a song I heard on the radio. It is funny the different outlooks people have from the same line.

Live Like You Were Dying

Should live like you were dying, it's the only sensible way
To ensure your salvation that will surely come someday
None of us knows for sure just how long we have here
But, if you live like you were dying, your future is secure

Must give your soul back to "The One" that created it
Really only on "loan" to you to find a spot it fits
The decision is all yours, you have a lifetime to find out
Whether will be the fires of hell, or for heaven to shout

Boy Scout motto says "Be Prepared," that's good advice
'Cause you never know when will be the end of your life
Only takes one big error in judgement to ruin your soul
Must seek His forgiveness right now to reach your goal

We all live, love and pray in this life given to us
Make sure praying's on your list or you will miss the bus
Remember the reason that God gave us this life we lead
Is to attain eternal salvation by His words we heed

The story behind the poem: I met a woman on the Internet once that seemed to think that because she loved God she couldn't love me too. This was my answer to her line of thinking.

True Love

True love is endless, as God ordained it should be
Love Him whole heartedly there is still room for me
A different kind of love, there is more than one kind
What you give to Him is Divine, mine meant to bind

We were put on this earth to enjoy this life we have
Man and woman were meant to join, never to halve
Prayers sent up to heaven always best done in pairs
God gives them special attention because He cares

To achieve eternal life in heaven should be your goal
And a help-mate to get you there, and save your soul
It's what we can give to each other that really counts
God blesses such a holy union in very great amounts

Just thought I would try and tell you how it really is
I may just be a lonesome cowboy, but my heart is His
Plenty of room left over in this very big heart of mine
To take good care of you for the rest of our time

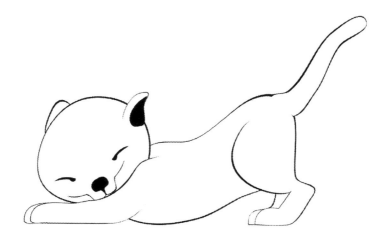

The story behind the poem: Robin told me happiness and peace of mind were all that she wanted and desired. I told her it was all in this book. All she had to do was to believe it, and practice it. I said that she should try love, because it works.

Happiness

Happiness, always within, we just need to get it out
Need to learn why we're here, what life's all about
Happiness is something we create inside ourselves
Is infused in our soul by God, that's where it delves

It may be a cute loving puppy or little fur-ball kitten
And with either one of these could well be smitten
Real love returned to you is such a wonderful thing
And, real happiness to you it will most surely bring

Be a caring friend, love even those you don't know
It will all come back ten-fold, make your heart glow
Give and you shall receive, it's always the best way
That's why we're all here, you will see that someday

When real love is your mate, that's special indeed
Because what you feel for them you have a need
Then the happiness created within goes on and on
Will turn your whole life into a beautiful love song

The story behind the poem: This is a story I first read in an email. It reminded me of me, so I converted it to a poem.

The Burning Ember

An old rancher there was, hadn't been to church in years
Didn't think that he needed to rub elbows with his peers
The pastor of a "Cowboy" church came to visit one night
To encourage him to attend services; to shed some light

They greeted at the door, then nothing more was said
The pastor sat down in an easy chair, laid back his head
There was a warmth from the fireplace, with tools nearby
They would both stare at it as the cool evening went by

The pastor picked up a burning ember from the hot fire
Placed it off to the side that the rancher could admire
Glowed for awhile, and then with one last flicker of light
Went out, laid there dead, of no use against the night

Then the pastor replaced the dead ember again in the fire
Absorbed the flames, and was burning with much desire
Then the pastor got up to leave, still hadn't said a word
The rancher shed a tear, the silent sermon he had heard

Said: "I will be attending your services next week, for sure
Under my saddle I will be removing that troublesome burr."
The rancher hadn't realized that his heart was all alone
Would have faith and friends and future for him to hone

The story behind the poem: I was upset, and besides that didn't know what to write about. My mind was a blank page.

A Blank Page

Not sure what I see, a blank page stares back at me
My emotions are in turmoil they just won't let me be
I think of all those I have helped along this week
With the answers to all their problems that they seek

The one with the real sticky problem is surely me
Don't have anyone that even understands, you see
How can I solve those problems I can't even define?
Can't talk to anyone that sees through eyes of mine

My heart was hurting like it never did before, it's sad
That a grown man, like me, could even hurt this bad
There are no easy answers, maybe no answers at all
About how to get out of this after I've taken the fall

Now she owns my heart, gave it away, don't you see?
She doesn't really want it but won't give it back to me
Now there's my sticky problem like a tree of thorns
Never had this much trouble since the day I was born

The story behind the poem: This poem has been rolling around in my head for several days now. I thought it might make a good movie. Then, I realized there was a movie made many, many years ago called "The Robe." I didn't see it but thought that it might have gone something like this.

The Robe

Whack, the nails were driven deep into His tender hands
By a Roman soldier named Kiafus; didn't know the Man
The sign placed over His head said: "King of the Jews"
He wondered why they crucified Him if this were true!

Then immediately He was lifted up and left there to die
The soldiers divided His garments, on the ground they lie
When they came to His outer robe, very beautiful it was
Seamlessly woven from top to bottom: caused a buzz

They decided not to tear it, but would cast lots instead
To see who would be the proud owner once He was dead
The winner would be Kiafus, this would be his lucky day
Wore the robe home: told his wife the lots ran his way

Kissed her gently on the cheek; very unusual for him
He felt like a completely new man, full of vigor and vim
He seemed to have a new attitude and outlook on things
He felt all the love and forgiveness coming from the King

The story behind the poem: I was driving my cab one morning and stopped in front of Safeway, having no ride. A dy-no-mite blonde walked by in a mini-skirt. I wrote this poem on a piece of paper on the roof of my cab while standing next to it. Inspiration can come from anywhere.

Beautiful Women

A lot of beautiful women in this world there are
It is poetry in slow motion, even better, by far
Their moves are so fluid and so full of grace
At times distracts from the beauty of their face

When I find the one that has that beauty inside
In her heart, mind and soul that she can't hide
This woman I choose to love, as it should be
Because I will know God has made her for me

It's been a long search, it lasted many years
Been through a lot of heartache and even tears
But now know who that one is at very long last
The one meant for me to make up for the past

Now that I have found her, must face the trial
She has been in another's arms all this while
This broken road of life God has truly blessed
Now He's trying me out, putting me to the test

The story behind the poem: My house has been cold all winter and I finally broke down and bought a heater. It brought to mind this poem.

Baby Jesus

Ice cycles cling to the rooftops lest they fall down and break
Wonder if the Baby Jesus was warm as He laid there awake?
Do you suppose that's the way it was when Jesus was born
Lying in a manger of hay with swaddling clothes to stay warm?

I wonder if His little mind knew that which brought Him here
That He'd be crucified to save the world, would it cause fear?
How painful it must be living your whole life knowing that
You'd be nailed to a cross and even whipped across the back

Maybe Our Heavenly Father had some mercy on Him after all
Didn't allow Him to know about this until the last curtain call
There are so many questions I want to ask when I get there
He will have an eternity to answer me, His wisdom to share

It's because of Him I will have this opportunity to attend
Just need my ducks in a row, my soul He will mend
How do you say thanks for a gift as magnificent as that
I will have an eternity to try, maybe give a little back

The story behind the poem: I was looking into the mirror one day, and knowing that she was always attracted to good looking guys, these thoughts came to mind.

The Mirror

Look into the mirror, wonder what looks back at me
There is more inside that which you don't even see
The real person is the heart and soul, without doubt
What good is only a handsome face to carry about?

Time you looked inside, see the real me that's there
Find the true love I feel for you that's forever to share
True beauty is in the eyes of the beholder, so they say
Always resides within, but can be seen plain as day

All you have to do, look at me, take your blinders off
Will find a love that is so true and very incredibly soft
Saw the beauty that resides within you a long time ago
Matches the beauty outside you are so fond to show

Have been blest with much beauty, within and without
Reason enough that you should praise Him and shout
My beauty resides within, in my writing, and caring ways
Would rather have that than a handsome face any day

The story behind the poem: I was reading a book that was explaining the differences between loving God and fearing God. It made sense. Eternity is a mind boggling concept.

Fear of God

Going to talk about something very unpleasant here
It's because your well being is held near and dear
Some preachers teach only of God's mercy and love
They forget about His justice: to fear Him from above

The fear of God was put into our hearts for a reason
So we would obey God's laws through the seasons
Love of God is not enough to keep us from falling
We need the fear of eternal punishment in our calling

Hell is fire and brimstone with that unbearable heat
Absolutely alone, with no one to ever again speak
The darkness is incredible, can't see into black space
Worms that never die eating the flesh from your face

A terribly, dark, horrible place to have to go someday
Maybe you had better tend to what you do and say?
Eternity can't be comprehended by our finite minds
Obey God's laws and fear Him for all your earthly time

The story behind the poem: It is Thanksgiving Day, and I am alone, but not really alone. I have my "Angel" in my mind, and in my heart. That is more than enough to be thankful for.

Robin

You have changed me for the better; changed me for good
The way you have affected me, no one but only you could
When I first saw your lovely face and that beautiful smile
My heart was forever taken and you knew it all the while

This gift from God you were able to bring out in me
I will carry forever to my grave, indeed for all of eternity
Seems I was gifted twice, first by God, then by you
Double blessing, I am sure; allows me to do what I do

You have opened me up like no one before you was able
To pour out my thoughts and feelings, put them on the table
Now this poem book, almost finished, just a little way to go
You will get a leather-bound copy, for my love to show

Now must use this gift, as instructed by Him, and by you
To show the world what real love is, that which is true
Will leave this legacy of love behind when I go from here
I will forever remember you and the times you were near

The story behind the poem: One day I just woke up and realized that in spite of all the poems, plaques and prayers I couldn't make Robin love me. Because I have a heart, I am a fool. But, I wouldn't have traded the experience for anything in this world.

The Fool

There's always a town drunk, and a town fool
And my little berg is no exception to that rule
In my own home place that fool would be me
'Cuz I'm in love with her as everyone can see

She had a longtime husband when we first met
And now it is a boyfriend she must get over yet
In her thoughts and dreams I don't even exist
Her sweet love is something I will surely miss

I tried to impress her with poems and plaques
Was like so much water falling off a duck's back
Her love vessel is clear full: can hold no more
Must wait until it's very empty that I may restore

I have prayed my prayer nine times each night
That maybe Saint Jude would show me the light
He solves impossible causes, they are his forte'
But, I will remain a fool still, until my dying day

The story behind the poem: I was just having rambling thoughts when this came to me. That happens to me a lot.

Breathless

Life is not measured only by the breaths you take in
But by the moments that leave you breathless within
When you find something that takes your breath away
You should embrace it, like a hug, that will last all day

A harvest moon above the lake, a baby learning to walk
A song heard on the radio that makes you hush the talk
An X-ray returned to you, no sign of the dread disease
Makes you want to give thanks to God, hit your knees

The birth of a new foal ranks up there with the best
There is something about new life, tear ducts it will test
To feel that new heart beating within is a God-sent gift
Tuck it all away deep inside, surely your spirits it will lift

Now, what do you suppose we are talking about here?
Those moments in your life that have brought you to tears
Has it been a long while since it has happened to you?
Maybe you should look within for your heart to renew?

The story behind the poem: It occurred to me that much in our lives is invisible. There is much that we must take on faith. Show me a man without faith, and I will show you the walking dead.

More Than What You See

There is more to life than what you see around you
There are dreams that you dream. isn't that really true?
You will "see" your dreams with your good night's sleep
And then forget them. 'cause they're not yours to keep

The best dreams by far are those you have while awake
That allows you to choose which ones of them to make
There once was a great man that said: "I have a dream"
And it came true for him because he believed. it seems

Every great action of merit is preceded by one thought
An invisible force that is stronger than anything bought
If you don't have dreams God has given you to do
How will you fulfill the destiny He has planned for you?

The key it would seem. to love others more than yourself
Love God above everything. for sharing all of His wealth
Heaven may be a dream too. but I know it's really there
'Cause God loves us all. and He has promised to share

The story behind the poem: A conversation I had with a friend prompted this poem. Of course, we were talking of young people.

Youth

Youth is always wasted on the very young, for sure
Better given to all the old timers that have endured
Their experiences and knowledge would fill a book
Wasted their own youth with the chances they took

Now much older and they, of course, know better
They tell the young ones how to do it to the letter
Guess God had a sense of humor with all of this
Wasted youth on young so the old could reminisce

Along this same line of thinking there's the brain
At fifteen or sixteen seems to be full to the crain
No room for more knowledge, already know it all
By about thirty five they are ready for that big fall

When we do know it all, like some of us have sung
Why can't we have the youth wasted when young?
If were to only know then what I have learned now
My youth would not have been wasted somehow

The story behind the poem: I have been wanting to write this for a long time but didn't know how. The word merchant was at a loss for words.

My Four Sons

I had four sons many, many years ago, it seems
My oldest one drowned when he was seventeen
Haven't seen the others in such a very long while
Dealing with their father seems to be such a trial

The three that are left have families of their own
They have no idea for them the love I have shown
Don't get a chance to see them, it's hard to share
The love I really feel and show how much I care

It's very difficult these thoughts to share with you
Because I have not been a good father, that's true
Lost them years ago in a "crash" that was severe
My mind was far gone, they didn't want to be near

Things are different now, my mind is in rare form
God gave it all back to me that I should be reborn
Now, if my children He would just give back to me
My mind would be at ease for the rest of eternity

The story behind the poem: For those of you that may not be familiar with what the Bible has to say about the second coming of Christ, I wrote this poem. You will find that it is very close to being Biblically correct.

Armageddon

Jesus will arrive on a great white horse with no name
Leading the armies of heaven to put the devil to shame
The antichrist, false prophets, and armies of the nations
Will all surrender their lives and in hell take their stations

He shall smite them in one day of battle with His sword
And the birds of the air will feast on them until gorged
Peace will reign on God's earth for one thousand years
There will be no wars, hatred, prejudice, crime or fear

All nations will beat their swords into plowshares
Of spears make pruning hooks; war they would not dare
Money system will be secure, with global prosperity
The saints of heaven and Jesus will rule for posterity

After one thousand years Satan will again be released
Rebels surround Jerusalem to make war like some beast
The fire of God will descend from heaven and devour
Devil will be cast into the lake of fire to forever cower

The story behind the poem: The only real time that any one of us has is right now. The sooner we realize this the better we will handle what God has given us.

Finding Yourself

Time: a God created thing, it takes up no space at all
An illusion that makes up the past and future on this ball
You need to live in the now: that's the only real place
Where you learn who you really are: look God in the face

The secret to successful living is to "die before you die"
And find that there is no real death, no reason to cry
Death is just a stripping away of all that is not you
Puts you back into the spirit world so you see God too

Time is past and future: we can only live right now
There's no greater obstacle to God than wasted time, anyhow
Lots of Love, Joy and Peace can be found within you inside
Quit living in the past and future: there's no time to bide

So, put your mind to rest and stop all those thoughts
Reach the stillness inside that can't even be bought
There you'll find Love, Joy and Peace and even better health
'Cause you will know that you will never again lose yourself

The story behind the poem: This poem was the culmination of several things that were going through my head. I hope it makes sense to you.

Impossible Dreams

Can those impossible dreams still be accomplished at last?
The ones you thought were forever gone, were in your past?
Now you see your chance, has resurrected itself once more
Now makes you wonder what's happening, what's in store?

Dreams never die, you just quit believing in them, you see?
They're always there with you, make you be all you can be
If you follow your God given dreams that He leads you to
You know you have accomplished your purpose here to do

Sometimes the difficulties seem near impossible to surmount
Might be your age, weight, gender or anything you can count
What you have to realize is these mountains are to climb
God has given them to you to resolve in your own time

If you don't at least try, might as well be dead, that's right
'Cause there is no hope for someone who can't follow the light
If dreams get away from you it's your own fault, by far
'Cuz you didn't hold tight enough to your own falling star

The story behind the poem: I got to thinking about going back home because I was lonely, and in great physical pain. This poem just rolled out through the pain and tears, it helped.

Options Are The Spirit Speaking

Sometimes, when your options run out it is a good sign
It means you should do something different, about time
The Spirit is guiding you that you make the right choice
So when the end is near you will be able to rejoice

Are you many miles from home, been a long time away?
Never had the courage to go back 'cuz you went astray?
Maybe it's time to seek comfort around family and friends
Family is the full circle: where it started, where it will end

How can you be lonely when there is family and friends?
Why don't you go home see what fences you can mend?
It might be your last chance, there's no way to know
God has given you strong ties your love you might show

Family is of only one blood, so is the whole human race
Can't even walk the street and say "stranger" to any face
If you have never been lonely just send a prayer to afar
He allowed your heart to acquire friends where you are

The story behind the poem: People need to realize that the accumulation of wealth is useless, except to help others. You can't take it with you.

A Legacy of Love

You will leave this world only with what you entered
No riches, real estate, cars or luggage are permitted
Have you ever seen a hearse with a luggage rack?
It is not needed because they are not coming back

It's what you leave behind you that really does count
A legacy of love, and friendship, in very great amounts
True love will last forever, and it transcends all time
It travels with you, inside your heart, soul and mind

You need to leave a part of you for others to share
Show them how much you love them and really care
With the legacy you leave you have but one chance
Will be your life's work, God will see it at a glance

Your reward will come for the good life you lead
Eternal happiness will be yours for your good deeds
Jesus said to follow Him on this quest for eternal life
End forever the sickness, pain, toil, trouble and strife

The story behind the poem: Got to thinking of the ranch I used to have and all the good things about it. One of the best was my dog. He was a wonderful animal and a good friend.

A Dog Named Blue

On my ranch I had a wonderful dog named "Blue"
He would get restless when the cows would moo
A real born cow-dog, a pure Blue Heeler he was
Liked to nip their noses and heels just because

I'd open the corral gate and give him a whistle
He'd race out to get them through the star thistle
He would round them all up and head them in
He would do the work better than several men

Had him a very long time, since he was a pup
And his backside I never once needed to whup
Then when he got older, got cancer in his eye
Got bigger than a tennis ball, soon he would die

Needed to put him to sleep, it had to be done
Just couldn't do it, neighbor shot him with a gun
Thank you for that my friend, wherever you are
You saved me from a lot of pain and grief, by far

The story behind the poem: I overheard a discussion on the measure of a man. Of course it didn't go anything at all like this poem. I thought I would set the record straight. Enjoy.

The Measure of a Man

The measure of a man is in the things he holds close
Holds God in his heart because He matters the most
Holds a tiny baby in his hands giving her the right start
Loves her oh so gently as he holds her to his heart

The measure of a man: that which he does for all others
Volunteers his time to help out because we're all brothers
On a rainy day helps an old woman get across the street
Holds her umbrella for her so she stays dry on her feet

The measure of a man: for him all nature to honor
God gave him this beauty for him to quietly ponder
He has great love for both his father and his mother
They gave him life: he wouldn't trade them for another

The measure of a man is how he treats God's little ones
Protects them with a careful eye while they play and run
Jesus said we should come to Him as simple as a child
Innocent, loving, trusting and with a heart meek and mild

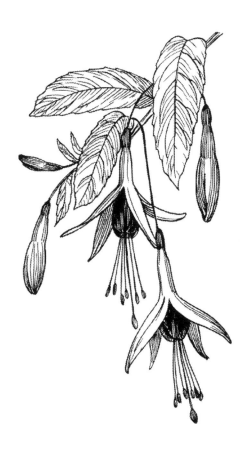

The story behind the poem: I like to use stories from the Bible once in a while. Jesus was a remarkable teacher and His parables were simple and easily understood.

Worry Not

Worry not about what you shall eat, or what you shall drink
Be concerned not about clothes to wear to cover skin of pink
Birds of air neither sow nor spin; gather into barns to keep
But, heavenly Father feeds the least of these while we sleep

Are you not more important than any birds of the air?
All you have to do is for your true allegiance to swear
The beautiful lilies of the field toil not; neither do they weave
Even Solomon in all his glory was not arrayed such as these

What He's trying to say, be concerned not by this earth
But by things that are eternal, such as your soul's rebirth
If we lived that way would be a pleasant place to be
We would all be there with Him, in heaven, for eternity

So the choice is all yours, has been since you were born
Live a life centered on earthly things or a righteous robe adorn
You can't even imagine the rewards from just doing it right
The option is hell; an eternity of suffering and black night

The story behind the poem: I heard a song on the radio and put a different twist to it. Something I have been thinking about anyway.

No Regrets

I'm going to hate myself in the morning, that's for sure
But I am going home tonight my self worth to ensure
Your beauty is overwhelming, you love to hug and kiss
And your sweet love is something I will surely miss

The problem is you are not "the one" in my dreams
Can't go any farther with it, it's not within my means
Don't believe in just doing sex, guess I rarely ever have
True love makes both souls into one never to halve

Some people get by and never even look for true love
Interested in fun and games, no thought of Him above
If it's heaven you seek need to get your priorities right
So you won't be ashamed if you reach heaven tonight

Sex was made for procreation, and to express true love
Anything less than that and you offend Him from above
So take care of that which you have when you go out
Better not to use it at all if you have any doubts

The story behind the poem: Perfection is always in the eyes of the beholder I am sure. A beautiful woman is determined by what's inside, not what's outside.

The Perfect Woman

You are indeed the perfect woman for me
There will be no more, as far as I can see
Many trials and tribulations to get this far
Has left my heart and soul with a big scar

You have healed me now, I can surely tell
My heart sings with joy and clear as a bell
You have touched my soul as none before
You filled my being right down to the core

Your beauty is much more than skin deep
Your soul shines, your heart mine to keep
How did I get so lucky? I haven't a clue
That God should allow me just to love you

You were made for me and I know that now
God sent to find me but I don't know how
The Power from way above shines on you
Hope to be worthy of your pure love too

The story behind the poem: I went for a walk in the quiet evening. The Spirit was talking to me, and I was listening.

Humility

Humility is a virtue that we can all use some more of
You need to realize the gifts you have are from above
Did you think it was all you inside that brain of yours?
God has blessed you with all of those gifts you store

You need to use them as He intended, don't you see?
Helping those who are less fortunate be all they can be
Will find helping others get their lives straightened out
It's your surest way to get to heaven, without any doubt

It's just another type of love, one of the better kinds
To share your gifts with people you know, it will bind
The personal rewards are great for that which you do
But the biggest reward is heaven that comes to you

Don't you think it's about time to open up your mind
Give some of it back to God for Him being so kind?
As with all types of love you can't give too much away
It will be returned to you a little bit more each day

The story behind the poem: Are you looking for answers in your life? Maybe you should look at love as a solution.

Love is The Answer

What is the big question that perplexes you right now?
You don't have an answer, your mind is not endowed
Maybe you should look at love, it seems to answer all
Love is the solution for all your problems big and small

Are you going through a divorce, or maybe lost a child?
Perhaps you lost your job, or home, make you go wild?
These are very small things in the grand scheme of life
Love can fill that void, help do away with the strife

You need to love God the most, without any reservation
Then you need to love yourself, you are worth salvation
Love those around you, even those strangers you meet
It will all come back to you, just lay at your feet

Love: the strongest force that God has endowed us with
Love can walk through heaps of fire for that single kiss
Love is all consuming as God ordained that it should be
Just remember that true love is coming, at least from me

The story behind the poem: A lot of people are confused with the difference between "falling in love," and true love. Maybe this will help.

Love Explained

"Falling in love," not really love at all, it would seem
Just fireworks, shooting stars and whistles that scream
Only a chemical, physical, sexual, emotional state it is
Created by God to ensure procreation for those of His

True love is really elusive, like most all of your dreams
Will strike when you least expect it, that it would seem
Really a matter of choice, one that you make everyday
And in the arms of this person you are destined to stay

You don't "try" true love, will find that it will try you
To see that you are worthy while God makes you new
That nice ring on your finger has no beginning nor end
It symbolizes eternity, where your soul He will send

So there you have it friend, the good, and the very best
Are you ready, at last, to put your heart to the test?
True love, a commitment you must make for all time
For better, for worse, while the bells of heaven chime

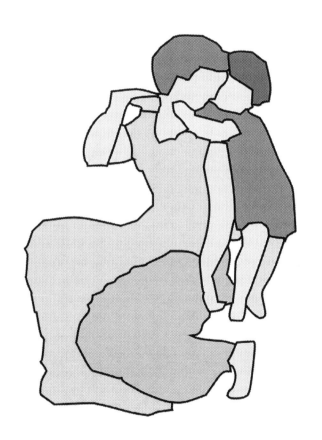

The story behind the poem: I met a woman today. She takes care of mentally handicapped adults and children. She is a very caring and loving woman, as was demonstrated by the hug she gave to one young man that I witnessed. She made me feel like I needed a hug too. She inspired this poem. My way of saying thanks for what she does.

Making a Difference

When you make a difference in lives of those you meet
You will fulfill your purpose here for time spent you seek
You must share all the gifts you have with those in need
Be kind to others, 'cuz you know your words they will heed

We're all here to help one another, seems like it to me
Will mend your soul to be of service to others, you see!
Lot of the time they don't know they're in need of you
Until you come along; make them see things that are true

Friends you will make that don't easily fall beside the road
For showing them the way life can be full, carry their load
The sadness that was residing within will be turned into joy
Then find someone else to help, don't let their antics annoy

The nicest result is the good things that often happen to you
Will make you a much better person for that which you do
You will leave the encounter feeling very good about yourself
Will feel like a million bucks; adding much to your wealth

The story behind the poem: I delivered the framed poems and the book to Marie today. She takes care of the mentally handicapped people. Her response was nothing less than overwhelming. I expected that from an "angel."

She Called Me An Angel

She called me an "angel" because of that which I did
I said: "No, you are the angel for helping these kids"
We both wept and embraced, as two friends should
It's hard to imagine we just met, it was so good

Isn't that the way our lives are really supposed to be?
Show one another the good in them, and them in me
She lightened my load the very first time I saw her
She made me yearn for a hug that would make me purr

Got my hug, many times over, would seem to me
She absolutely made my day by her responses, you see?
God's reward for the work He chose me to do for life
Makes the effort all worth while, eliminates all the strife

If I could meet someone like this every day that I live
I would be so enormously blest by the poems I give
Am here to "touch" others, make a difference in their lives
Seems they end up touching me and make my heart rise

Heb. 13:2 Be not forgetful to entertain strangers:
For thereby some have entertained angels unawares.

The story behind the poem: I was sitting on the porch drinking a cup of coffee and watching the leaves come down. Then, I went inside and wrote this poem.

Autumn

The leaves are falling, they make a rustling sound
In colors of brown and gold, as they fall to the ground
The litter covers many lawns and fields close at hand
Fall arrives, once again, over this big wondrous land

Maybe it's time for reflection on this life you have led
Might be the autumn of your life, may soon be dead
Don't you think it's about time to make peace with God
'Fore they bury you, for all time in the cold, cold sod?

When you look back on all the autumns you've had
Make sure to see joyful times, no reason to be sad
This life as we know it will end, 'twas destined to be
So that we may enjoy God's heaven for all eternity

There is still time to repair damage done in your life
God is all forgiving, His Son payed forever the price
The end is the beginning, and the beginning the end
Repair the autumn of life, so to heaven He will send

The story behind the poem: Light is so fast it travels almost six trillion miles in a year. The sun provides us with light, heat and a reason to get up in the morning. Light does other marvelous things for us as well, as you will see in this poem.

The Light of Life

Light, bright light, it's job is to keep darkness from our sight
The only single thing that can overcome the darkness is light
The light falls on the good, the bad: unjust and the just
It has no discrimination: just trying to redeem us before dust

The Light: spiritual illumination of this world by Truth Divine
Jesus said: "I am the light of the world": that's our sign
Where there is light there will be shadows creeping about
Shadows: just darkness trying to gain a foothold no doubt

Surrender is yielding to, rather than opposing, the flow of life
You need God in your life to eliminate all of the strife
"He that follows Me shall not walk in darkness." Jesus said
"But shall have the light of life" to guide his way instead

Given a choice between dark and light, which would it be?
You would choose the Light of Life it would seem to me
Then when you see the city brightly lit up at night
You will smile 'cuz you will be shining with Inner Light

The Story Behind The Poem: It is hard to explain what happens to you when you are reborn. It is a very different experience. I hope this poem will give you a little insight.

A Child of God

I am a child of God, this is ever so plain for all to see
Am so grateful for what The Holy Spirit has done for me
He's infused my soul with understanding, knowledge and love
All this, and even much more, comes from our God above

When you become a child of God, you gain new insight
You see many situations where you might shed some light
You gain a new set of ears too, to really hear others pain
To listen to them very carefully and a new friend gain

The biggest thing you gain is love for everyone's soul
Treat everyone as your brother or sister, that's your goal
As a child of God you will love The Father the most
He has earned it by creating you, and the heavenly host

To be a chosen child of God is an incredible honor
All of the gifts you gain you will need to ponder
All it takes is surrendering yourself completely to God
After all, He's the Almighty One that made you from sod

The story behind the poem: Here I sit, all racked with pain because my back is out of place. I can only type a few letters at a time. Then this poem came to me, what was I supposed to do? I wrote it, it just took a while. Merry Christmas.

Merry Christmas Jesus

A bright star is now shining from high above
Shows three kings The One they should love
They bring gifts: gold, frankincense and myrrh
To honor Baby Jesus, He likes them for sure

The little drummer boy plays Him a lovely tune
A soft, gentle one because it will be light soon
The Mother of God has a halo about her head
To match the one Baby Jesus has, so it's said

The shepherds gather around to see this sight
Knowing never again will there be such a night
Strains of "Oh Holy Night" fill the crisp, cool air
Sung by a chorus of angels that came to share

The sheep, oxen and camels quietly stand by
They have never seen a Baby that didn't cry
Such a Holy Night world will never again see
The night that Jesus was born to set us all free

The story behind the poem: "The poet; but a dreamer who plays with words, touches your heart, then flies away like a bird. He can reveal your soul, make you see yourself, his job done, puts his heart back on the shelf."

A Poet

There once was a poet that I would get to know well
He was my father's son, my brother's brother, do tell
He used to write of trivial things, about romance stuff
Then a Voice spoke in his ear, saying that is enough

It was a gentle Voice at first, more forceful over time
Saying "You need to write of Me in all those rhymes"
He learned of his calling; little bit at a time it seems
Now is just trying to do that which God has deemed

Didn't pretend to be a poet with lots of talent, you know?
Just trying to ply his trade, for God his love to show
God supplies the ideas for these poems all of the time
He tries to write them down and make them all rhyme

When God is at your side how can you ever go wrong?
He says the next step will be to turn them into songs
Feels very blest that God gave this gift of love to us
He listens very carefully to the Voice, so as not to hush

The story behind the poem: Being an old farm boy from way back I can really appreciate this parable. It may give you some food for thought as well.

The Sower

When a sower went out to sow, some fell by the wayside
They were eaten by the fowls of the air; seeds couldn't hide
Some fell on stony ground where there was not much earth
Immediately sprang up because they had no depth since birth

When the sun came up, were scorched, and severely burned
Because they had no root they withered away, so I've learned
Some fell among the thorns that grew up and choked them
No fruit would be yielded by seeds growing in light so dim

Yet others did fall on good ground and yielded much. I'm told
Some thirty, and some sixty, and some even a hundred fold
The seeds are The Word of God falling on our ears
The wayside is where the devil takes them as fast as fear

The stony ground receives The Word with all gladness
But has no root within themselves to sustain in sadness
The ones surrounded by thorns: choked by riches and lusts
Those on good ground? let's pray they're the rest of us

The story behind the poem: You need the portal of silence to get inside yourself. Have you ever noticed that monks and monasteries are always located in the quiet mountains?

Silence

Silence is golden: have you ever thought about why?
No noise in your ear, just a beautiful clear, blue sky
When you give your attention to the silence outside
It creates a portal to silence within, for you to abide

All sounds are born of silence, die into silence again
Where there is no silence at all you can't get within
The silence within is where God chooses to dwell
True Love, wisdom and creativity reside there as well

Silence is the one thing that resembles God the most
He's in and around all things in this vast cosmos
Silence: an absence of sound: a sign of His presence
It must be that way because silence is His essence

So when you pray to God, better to do so in silence
Find a place far away from all noise and violence
And, while you're inside yourself, look around awhile
Find the True Love inside: come to Him as a child

The story behind the poem: I was sitting outside one evening, just before sunset, watching the beautiful red clouds in the sky. Then this poem just came to me.

I See God

I see God in the face of that little girl's toothless grin
The one that says your heart I will surely always win
I see God pushing a shopping cart on a downtown street
Wearing ragged clothes and with no shoes on her feet

I see God in the majestic mountains surrounding our valley
Snow covered peaks that draw skiers to the outdoor rally
I see God riding in a wheelchair with legs twisted and bent
Just trying his best to deal with that which life has sent

I see God lying there on that big sterile hospital Gurney
Life oozing out of him as he prepares for his journey
I see God at the coast where the oceans always roar
Never ending, wave after wave, while the seagulls soar

I see God in the sky, when the clouds turn bright red
And in the doe protecting her fawn as she poses her head
I even see God in the air that's life given to breathe
Must see Him up close, in person, as this body I leave

The story behind the poem: I am cold, and I am wet, but my heart is warm. That is because I know you will be reading this and it will make a difference in your life. It has in mine.

Thoughts

There is something inside of me that is trying to get out
I don't know what it is, but makes me scream and shout
Thought that if I just started writing maybe it would surface
Let me know that my writing, at least, served a purpose

Sometimes my writing makes no sense to anyone but me
That's because I am the one feeling the feeling, you see?
If you are able to understand and appreciate what I write
Then will know you are a sensitive person, a lot of insight

Lots of people write poetry, usually only when they're sad
Would think the poems would be better when they're glad
People need to feel the wonderful joy that's created within
"Touching" your fellow brothers and sisters, you both win

I have tried to convey true thoughts and feelings thruout
That you might connect with me, see what life's all about
If I have succeeded will send my thanks to heaven above
Knowing He was the reason, because God is True Love

The story behind the poem: I started this poem a month or more ago. Tonight I wrote the last two verses. I don't very often do it that way, but there must be a reason for it.

If Jesus Was a Poet

If Jesus was a poet would have said things in rhyme
May not have been the same but it would be just fine
The poet is hindered by which words he chooses
Trying to make them sound right to the end users

My God has instilled in me the ability to teach others
He has chosen poems for me to instruct my brothers
I am following the thoughts that He put into my mind
Trying to fulfill His Holy Will and bring you my rhymes

If you're to learn the meaning of these poems of mine
Will find it necessary to see, and read between the lines
Some thoughts are deep and will make you ponder a lot
Put them into your mind for answers you have sought

If you get the answers you're looking for in this life
Then you will learn how to eliminate most of the strife
Then my job as a simple poet will have been well spent
You will know that these poems are from heaven sent

The story behind the poem: I don't think the good traits in us are stressed enough in elementary schools. Things like loyalty, humility, honesty, justice and the like should receive utmost importance in the classroom.

Loyalty

Loyalty can't ever be demanded, has to be earned, no doubt
By the respect you show others and mountains you surmount
If you always keep your word, and tell it like it is
They'll respect you for who you are, even that which is His

You should be loyal to others, well as them loyal to you
Because we are all brothers and sisters, of course that's true
This life without loyalty, would be such a grind, seems to me
Who then would you look up to, like them want to be?

Not even God, in all His greatness, demanded loyalty from us
Gave us a free will to choose, and even allowed us to cuss
If that's not freedom of choice I don't know what is
'Cuz if anyone could have demanded loyalty, the right is His

You see, loyalty is earned by that which you do for others
God instilled that in you and me, as well as our brothers
Be loyal to God, because His Son has now saved the day
That you might have a chance to choose your own way

The story behind the poem: I am sure you have heard the story about taking a trip and never leaving the farm. It was even put to music. That was drug induced. This is not. And, this has no downside.

The Journey Within

Do you like to take vacations or go on long trips?
When you get home do you feel let down a bit?
A common problem for most of us, I'm very sure
Is getting back on track after the vacations lure

Maybe you should try a shorter trip; the one inside
Will be the most life changing journey you will abide
It only takes one step to reach the "stillness" within
Will be the most loving, peaceful place you've been

There are no letdowns going to a place such as this
Why would you want to leave? It's full of such bliss
Leave your troubles there because there is no time
To ponder them and have them work on your mind

To open the door you must first cease all thought
About things you must do and things you bought
Focus on the space that's between your breaths
All thinking will stop and you can put it to the test

The story behind the poem: Something happened in my abode last night that triggered this poem. It is really odd the things that inspire me to write.

Snowflakes On The Floor

Snowflakes on the floor, because there's a hole in the roof
A hole in my heart as well, although I have no proof
When things are not going well, and get way out of hand
Raise your eyes to heaven, see if it's part of God's plan

There's always reasons for things to turn out the way they do
Most times it is your own fault, isn't that nearly always true?
Then there's those circumstances you have little control over
Small mountains you need to climb before you see the clover

"The end justifies the means," that I have often heard before
But think the means must be good, 'cuz He is keeping score
Where is the pride, the real joy, in something not done right?
Even though you may be counting the money until early light

Guess what I am trying to say, have said many times before
Must lead a life of love, and respect, to open heaven's door
God is waiting for you, with outstretched arms, seems to me
To show His love and caring for being all you can be

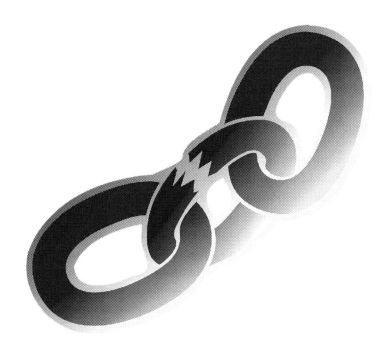

The story behind the poem: Broken trust hurts the offender more than the offended. Why not eliminate the pain you are causing them and yourself?

Trust

Trust is something that must be earned in this life
But, given freely by friends, family and even your wife
They assume you are trustworthy, until proven wrong
Then rebuilding trust must be started before to long

You must earn it back by the things you do and say
You must realize you can't have everything your way
You have to show them, for them you really do care
You have to show them true love you need to share

You also must put unlimited trust in our Almighty God
Because He has already earned it, making us from sod
The trust you put in God is never, ever put to waste
You should never forget that in this life's bizarre haste

He's asked us to surrender ourselves completely to Him
Trust Him to care for us here and when eternity begins
Enjoy peace and happiness beyond your wildest dreams
As you become a chosen member of our God's team

The story behind the poem: I was lying in the Nevada desert one summer night when this poem came to me. What an awesome sky!

Cool Sand

Cool sand touches my back: look up at the stars
Surely are a long way off, I wonder just how far?
This vastness of creation, no small miracle to see
Where do I fit in, what has God planned for me?

No woman has shown up just to hold my hand
I guess I'll just lay here on this cool, cool sand
How long can it take to find that one true love?
That's forever blessed by The Hand from above

Thought I had found her, but she didn't find me
Failed to look inside her heart, see her eternity
Now she is wandering about planting the seeds
And expects to harvest a love to fulfill her needs

That which you sow you will surely always reap
Make sure the seeds you plant you want to keep
Sometimes the best ones died, or withered away
'Cuz you were busy letting your heart run astray

The story behind the poem: A man I met said I had to write of the future. I don't know if this is what he meant, or not. Seems like the future to me.

Getting to Heaven

I believe in Jesus, He is the Great Lord
Said: "The Word is mightier than the sword"
Wisdom abounds in these words of His
Taught us love, fills our hearts with sizz

I say what I feel, try to keep it all correct
And will do this for as long as I'm erect
Gave me the thoughts I share with you
Now it's your doing to find the truth too

I'm an old cowboy, trying to make a living
Doing the best I can with what was given
Should strive to find out why we are here
Show God we're trying His laws to adhere

Guess I will know if it's been worthwhile
When my name arrives up there in style
When displayed on the Gates of Heaven
Will have arrived, can now join the Seven

The story behind the poem: This is something Jesus spoke of. Your rewards can be from here or heaven, your choice. Maybe you should think about making your gift count for eternity?

Alms

When you give alms do so quietly, if you please
Without trumpets blaring that others might see
Your reward will be earthly, or from God above
Depends on who sees it, friends, or Him we love

To give in secret will always make your day
They know not from where it comes anyway
They will look gleefully around to find the one
And with their hearts they will love everyone

You'll not only make their day but yours as well
God will love you and ring heaven's bells
I'm sure this is all He would like it to be
Secret gifts given to all others by you and me

So you see your gift serves several good uses
Helping those in need and eliminates excuses
So why don't you try and give all you can
Give gifts to all others according to God's plan

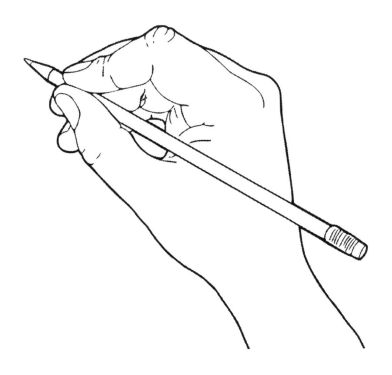

The story behind the poem: I tried to write several things with no success. So, I thought I would write about poems. Hope you don't mind.

Poems

For poems to mean anything there must be a lot of love
You also need cadence, rhythm in addition to the above
It's paramount, of course, that the reader be involved too
Must shed tears of pure joy when the poem gets to you

To appreciate a poem it needs to connect with you inside
You need to "find" yourself in it, know you can't hide
If the poem should become "you," both within and without
I will know I have touched you and have reason to shout

These are the kinds of poems I try very hard to write
The ones that touch your soul, make you see a new light
If I've succeeded in this effort will be a happy man
Guess you could say I tried to follow my God's plan

Will continue that which I'm able as long as I may live
For as long as God gives me the inspiration, then I'll give
Have found my calling in this very long life we lead
It's all up to you to find the words you should heed

The story behind the poem: I had a conversation with an architect the other day. He said he designed homes. I said he designed houses. We had quite a discussion about it.

The Architect

Who do you suppose is the greatest architect that ever was?
Surely it must be our God, because of the things He does
Who could ever imagine stalactites hanging there in a cave
Or the gravitational pull of the moon controlling every wave?

The clouds in the sky seem so simple, ever changing they are
The stars that shine every night for us, brilliant lights from afar
The moon and the planets hold steady to their fixed courses
What holds all these in place? It must be God's great forces

A house built by an architect, only a wooden shell at best
To make a home love must be added, to pass the test
Without love, it's only a house, and there are many of these
Add love, and you have a home, the owners have the keys

As with most everything else, the answer seems to be love
Love from our Heavenly Father, or love sent to Him above
Of course, there's love between all of us living here too
And just so you understand, am sending all my love to you

The story behind the poem: This is yet another poem that came from a story spoken by Jesus. I hope He doesn't mind that I borrowed it.

The Mouth

It's not that which goes into the mouth that defiles a man
But that which comes out of the mouth: defiles if it can
That which you eat goes from the mouth to the belly inside
That which you speak comes from the heart: others to abide

Out of the heart proceeds evil thoughts that are inside of
us About murders, thefts, fornication, adultery: we even cuss
We bare false witness, and blaspheme God's Holy Name
Seems there's never any end to our mouths bringing shame

Don't you think it's about time to become consciously aware
Of that which comes out of your mouth, like when you swear?
A person that curses a lot, just showing their own ignorance
For lack of learning a vocabulary they would find a hindrance

So be careful with your thoughts, and think before you speak
You will be judged for every word spoken your heart keeps
Your every word, thought, action and motive will be judged
So you'd better let God in, then your life He can nudge

The story behind the poem: I watched television for a few minutes this morning. I saw something on it that triggered this poem. It just rolled out, as usual.

Pain

The pain people feel is very, very real to them
It's the little speed bumps in life given by Him
He's testing you, seeing what you're made of
Just His way of giving and expressing His love

Some people crippled, have cancer uncured
Some have a lost love that must be endured
There are those with lost sight, unable to see
"See" with their heart, better than you and me

Then there is my oldest son, taken one June
Still don't know why, maybe will someday soon
It's not for us to question the reasons why
They will all become clear to us when we die

He is a just God, and of this am very sure
Your rewards will be great for all you endure
You just have to keep the faith, believe in Him
For all He is trying to do is your soul to mend

The story behind the poem: Every year at Christmas time I see this. It really irritates me to no end. Here is my answer to it.

Xmas

Seeing Xmas for Christmas really irritates me the most
It's like taking the "Holy" out of the very Holy Ghost
A pagan ritual I'm sure, least seems like it to me
Heathens replace Christ with an "X", there for all to see

Christ is the reason for the season, or didn't you know?
Was born on this day, His love, the whole world to show
Santa, reindeer and elves don't mean that much squat
Just there so you feel good about presents you bought

Try giving some of yourself, do a kindness to a stranger
And think of Him, The Babe, lying there in the manger
Christmas will take on a whole new, different meaning
You will find real love is what you will be gleaning

Let's put Christ back into Christmas where He belongs
And sing praises and hymns as our Christmas songs
Go to church when you can, but especially on this day
Show God that you care with the respect that you pay

The story behind the poem: I was just sitting here enjoying my new electric heater when this thought suddenly came to mind.

Love Is Electric

Electricity is totally useless if it's lying there in that line
Until you plug into it with something that uses it just fine
Now you can cook, clean and even heat your home too
When the days are hot, cool it a few degrees for you

Love is the same way, it's about everywhere you've been
Doesn't do you any good, of course, if you're not plugged in
You have to open your heart that your love might show
Will do incredible things for you, how do you think I know?

The strongest force ever created by God: real true love
That's because it comes from Him, from way up above
You just have to give it, then will be given on queue
If you really love others they will in return love you

It's all so incredibly simple, there are no moving parts
The only necessary ingredient is that you have a heart
Just try and give your heart away, I'll even dare you to
Know you can't do it because it will come back to you

The story behind the poem: Recently I have had an extremely severe attack of back pain that lasted over 20 days. Doctors and hospitals couldn't do a thing with it. No drugs were helping at all. They just gave up and sent me home. So, I put it into His hands, what else could I do? (P.S. It worked!)

Jesus, Take The Tiller

Please Jesus, take the tiller. I can't see anymore
The tears from all this pain are hiding the shores
Haven't slept in so long can't remember the days
My brain's no help at all, as it's been in a haze

I know You are around, place Your hand on mine
Steer this boat around the rocks, I will be just fine
Just need to lay my head on Your chest for awhile
And have You show me how to overcome this trial

We all have limits and I have surely reached mine
I need Your help or I'll never survive it this time
Have much work to do that You have asked of me
How do You expect me to obey if I can't even see?

Your obedient servant doing that which You asked
It seems the conditions create an impossible task
Is there something that I'm missing, unable to see?
Of course: faith in You, how big a fool can I be?

The story behind the poem: I have a brother that has "looked out" for me all my life. And, a brother-in-law for the past 20 years, or more. These men I shall not forget.

This Brother of Mine

What is a real brother? Let me tell you, so you know
He is the one that stands beside me his love to show
When no one else is there he is always near at hand
He is always there helping me up that I might stand

Sometimes I must put up with the abuse in his voice
But all he's trying to do: give me a meaningful choice
Have a brother-in-law, more like a real brother to me
Has stood beside and allowed me to be all I can be

Without them in my life, I would surely be a big mess
They don't often express it, but "hear" the love, no less
Am very much thankful to have brothers such as these
They will find the errors of my ways, if you will please

I have been blessed with brothers in this life of mine
Seems they are always arriving just in the nick of time
My biggest wish would be that they would really know
Someday I could repay them with the love I show

The story behind the poem: This poem is dedicated to the woman that had the most dramatic effect on my entire life. I can't let a book of love get by without paying tribute to her. She was my first love.

The Mother of My Children

When I was a very young man, all backward, and even shy
Would meet a woman soon to become the apple of my eye
Fell in love with her, she was everything I had ever dreamed
A gift straight from God, at least that's what it had seemed

She gave me four sons, there was nothing more I could ask
And if that wasn't enough, chose me as an even bigger task
Seems, that for everything I did, and everything I built
Said: "Gee Dave, you do good work," filled me to the hilt

My confidence grew in leaps and bounds, seems to me
She allowed me to grow up into the man you now see
Then, as cruel fate would have it, our hearts got torn apart
A piece of mine stayed behind because that was the start

True love still abides in me, echoing through my mind
About how it might have been if I had taken the time
The only single big regret that I still carry around with me
Not showing her true love, so the real me she might see

The story behind the poem: It is curious how some things just never leave your mind, even after twenty five years. I shed many tears when I wrote this poem just thinking about all the wonderful and loving times I was allowed to share with this woman.

Remember When

Remember when we danced the night away and fell in love?
Feet didn't even touch the floor, as if lifted by heaven above
Remember when we walked in Lithia park one glorious day?
With your little brothers and sisters in tow, hard at play

Remember when we hugged and kissed one moonlit night?
On the arched bridge over the creek; held each other tight
Remember when I asked you to marry me, and you said yes?
Just knew the rest of our lives would be heaven blessed

Remember when He gave us four sons? It was all we asked
Gave us a chance to raise them, and complete our task
Remember when an angel came and took our first born son?
Carried him up to heaven because his life here was done

Remember when I tried to be a good husband and father too?
Tried to love you and the boys all those years too few
Remember when we used to hold hands and walk in step?
When our love was still young, and promises still kept

The story behind the poem: I was driving home today thinking about the woman I needed in my life. This poem came crashing into my brain, as it usually does.

The Woman I Choose

The woman I choose to love will be ever so kind
She will always be helping others so we will bind
Will fill my heart and soul as it always should be
With love and compassion: wants to be with me

There will be no one else in this whole life of hers
That can fill her up without using diamonds or furs
I am what I am. she'll have to learn to accept that
She will find true love. I will show her where it's at

Will adore her as no other. like never, ever before
Must learn to trust me because eternity's in store
I will never, ever be unfaithful, or treat her unkind
Must always reside together and be of one mind

Want for all our time to become one with her
What God intended when He made love for sure
He meant two to become one. the rest of our lives
So we can both go to heaven. for this I shall strive

The story behind the poem: This poem occurred to me as I was driving home from town one day. I was thinking about the ocean, and the woman I would like to be there with.

One More Day

All that I could ever ask, have one more day with you
Watch the sunset over the ocean, the water so blue
This is my dream, one day, one night, to forever last
Then could get on with my life, memory in stone cast

The moon shines brightly, bouncing off of the waves
Like a thousand points of light, startling to the gaze
Soloman in all of his glory, not arrayed such as this
God did all in a heartbeat, a breath He did not miss

We would eat crab and steak, by the light of the fire
Drink a bottle of vintage wine, relax, until bodies tire
Then the darkness closes about us, light fog rolls in
Would head back to our hot tub, where fun begins

Days end would arrive, would get down on my knees
Pray to God for one more day so you I can please
Will need just one more day so not to lose touch
Tomorrow, will ask for it again; I love you this much

The story behind the poem: I am a Manic Depressive. I had a very severe "crash" in 1979, lost about 75% of my memory, could barely read and barely write. It took twenty long, hard years to get it all back, against 1000 to1 odds the doctor said. As I look back, I think it was all God's doing. He was rearranging my brain because He didn't like the way the old one worked.

A Manic Depressive

Happened in the winter of nineteen seventy nine
There was no clue I was about to lose my mind
Came out of nowhere with a "crash", so severe
Lost my wife, family, ranch and everything dear

The Hand of God would strike a severe blow
So that a new mind set I would have to show
The rebuilding would take twenty years or more
Worth the wait, changed me right to the core

Now I help all those in trouble, so it would seem
Use my poetry and insight the way God deems
Think this is the way He has meant it to be
He's shown me the road I should travel, you see

Now I want to live, and love, a good long while
To pay back for all those years I acted as a child
Now that my mind's mature and responding well
Look forward to heaven, don't even think of hell

The story behind the poem: I was sitting at home one night when I heard a song come on the radio. It inspired this poem right on the spot. There was a woman on my mind that wouldn't let me go.

A Mountain

God will not give me a mountain that I can't climb
I'd wondered a lot about that when I lost my mind
Over the years He cleansed it and returned it to me
Free of guilt, fear, doubt and all things bad, you see

He knows what He is doing, I'm so very sure of that
We have to trust Him, let Him show it by His acts
He loves us all, that's so easy for us to see
Just have to believe in Him, as He does in you and me

Now it is a woman that won't leave my mind alone
Someone to share my life, become one in my home
It's been a very long time without anyone for me
Have spent my forty years in the desert, you see?

I am ready for her, if He will show me the way
To join her heart with mine, get to heaven someday
Will be her heaven on earth I can promise you that
If He'll give me a chance to show her where it's at

The story behind the poem: I have always liked this story, probably because of my name. It serves two purposes as you will see. The story of two young men named David, him and me.

David and Goliath

The Philistines approached the Israelites, led by Saul
Had with them a giant named Goliath, six cubits tall
With a brass helmet, coat of mail, sword and spear too
Dared the Israelites to send someone out; battle to do

Young lad named David volunteered for the tough job
Armed with nothing but a leather sling and a love of God
As they approached each other, David his sling drew
Put a smooth rock in it and at Goliath's head threw

Loud "thunk" rang out, in Goliath's head the rock stuck
He fell hard to the ground; seems he forgot to duck
David ran to Goliath, cut his head off with his sword
Presented it to the King of Israel, received his reward

The Goliath in my life is Manic Depression, you see!
God gave me the sling and rock that overcame adversity
My brain went from mentally imbalanced to working great
A miracle of God's doing, to save me from my fate

The story behind the poem: I was in a great deal of pain, slightly delirious, when this poem came. I had to print it many times because tears kept washing the ink from the paper.

He Thought He Was Tough

There was a young man, very strong, and in his prime
Rode a Harley: always wore a knife, and a gun at times
He was raised on welfare: then he started stealing stuff
Filled with pride and arrogance: and he thought he was tough

Over the years he got married, had a lovely family too
God gave him four sons, and a wife: his work to do
Last son came by Caesarean: on her it was very rough
The scar lasted a lifetime: and he thought he was tough

Until a piece of land came, with his father-in-law's help
To raise beeves, hogs and children: a notch in his belt
Manic Depression hit, everything was gone: it was enough
His wife raised the children: and he thought he was tough

God sent a vision to him: to comprehend: and to see
Jesus' body, all covered in blood, shed for you and me
Scroll of my sins rolled out from the cross to my cuff
Each one blotted out with blood: and I thought He was tough

He was hanging there, but I couldn't see His face clearly
'Cause I was the thief on the cross behind: in Hell, nearly
Then Jesus said to me: "Love's the toughest thing, you see?"
"Sins are forgiven: In Paradise this day, with Me, you will be"

The story behind the poem: I feel honored to be allowed to bring you this book. I couldn't have done it alone.

Thank You

Thank you sweet Jesus, for allowing me to finish this book
Your love, caring and inspiration infused in my soul it took
Short time ago I wasn't even a writer, much less a poet
Now you have gifted me with the inspiration and I know it

The words seem to flow like they were Your own thoughts
Not a dictionary nor a thesaurus have I ever even bought
Tried to write down those words You have given to me
That the whole world might enjoy them, there for all to see

Lost my mind many years ago, this of course, You know
Gave me this gift as a way for Your love to show
Trying to do with it as You would like me to do
How will I ever be able to say many thanks to You?

Guess the only answer, make use of gifts that are given
We all have gifts from God to practice while we're livin'
You need to find your gifts and make good use of them
God gave them to you so you could then honor Him

The story behind the poem: Just one last poem for you, until I write volume two, of course. I hope these poems affected you in a positive way, that is all I could ever ask. They are all true in spirit, and told from the heart, from me to you.

Goodbye for Now

You have read this very far and now know me well
And the story about my loves, to you, I tried to tell
You have peered right inside my very heart and soul
And to open up to you was my most important goal

You can learn a lot from these poems as presented
Mold it into your life, make use of them as permitted
Take good advice from someone been around awhile
From experience, and others, must learn about trials

We don't need to live all, find the lessons life teaches
Just love God, into your innermost being He reaches
Cost everything in life that was of some value to me
Including my mind, then He gave it all back, you see?

There are only two given things that I never once lost
My faith in God, and in myself, to rise above the cost
Now I have arrived at this place He allowed me to be
The only wish I have left: His wonderful face to see

"Love is patient, love is kind. It does not envy, it does not boast, it is not proud. It is not rude, it is not self seeking, it is not easily angered, it keeps no record of wrongs. Love does not delight in evil but rejoices with the truth. It always protects, always trusts, always hopes, always preserves."

1 Corinthians 13:4-7, NIV

Jesus summed it up in two sentences when He said:

"This is My commandment, that you love one another as I have loved you. Greater love hath no man than this, that a man lay down his life for his friends."

John 15:12-13, KJV

The best use of life is love
The best expression of love is time
The best time to love is now

Rick Warren, The Purpose Driven Life, Zondervan Publishing

Index of Poems

Printed in the United States
By Bookmasters